W0186548

Inhalt

Allgemeiner Teil

Reihenkonzept Das Heft *India* ist ein Themenheft aus der Reihe „Abi Workshop Englisch". Diese Reihe bietet eine Sammlung von Themen- und Methodenheften, die speziell auf die Erfordernisse der G 8-Oberstufe und der zentralen Abiturprüfung ausgerichtet sind und ohne den Einsatz eines Oberstufen-Lehrwerks eine gründliche Vorbereitung des Abiturs gewährleisten. Während die

Methodenhefte Methodenhefte konsequent methoden- und kompetenzorientiert sind, bieten die Themenhefte einen landeskundlich-interkulturell ausgerichteten Überblick über ein relevantes Abiturthema.

Themenhefte Im Themenheft *India* sind die konzeptionellen Neuerungen der Reihe „Abi Workshop Englisch" auf folgende Weise realisiert:

Dokumenten CD-ROM

CD-ROM Auf der Dokumenten CD-ROM sind die Hörtexte, die Filmsequenzen und die *Vocabulary sheets* enthalten. Dadurch, dass die CD-ROM den Schülern und Schülerinnen (künftig: S) und Lehrern und Lehrerinnen (künftig: L) gleichermaßen zur Verfügung steht, können wichtige Lernbereiche deutlich intensiver behandelt werden als bisher. Für die S besteht die Möglichkeit zur Nachbereitung der Lernbereiche Hörverstehen bzw. Hör-/Sehverstehen sowie zu einer systematischen selbstständigen Wortschatzarbeit in der Oberstufe. Für die L bietet sich die Gelegenheit, diese Lernbereiche in die Unterrichtsvorbereitung durch die S einzubeziehen und sie zusätzlich auch für Hausaufgaben zu nutzen. Das Themenheft *India* enthält dementsprechend ausführliche Aufgabenstellungen.

Hör-/ Sehverstehen Für die weitere Schulung des Hör-/Sehverstehens stehen fünf Videoclips zur Verfügung, die mit einem ausführlichen Aufgabenapparat im Schülerheft versehen sind. Die Benutzung der Filmausschnitte im Klassenzimmer ist ausdrücklich gestattet. Darüber hinaus enthält das Themenheft *India* zahlreiche Aufgaben und Online-Links, sodass Hör-/Sehverstehen ohne die üblichen Probleme bei der Materialbeschaffung möglich ist. Insgesamt wird die Behandlung dieses Lernbereichs erheblich ausgeweitet und intensiviert.

Vokabelkonzept Das Themenheft *India* ermöglicht den S eine systematische und erfolgsorientierte Wortschatzarbeit in der Oberstufe, die eine optimale Vorbereitung auf das Abitur gewährleistet. Dazu wurde die Vokabelarbeit folgendermaßen organisiert:

Wortschatz im Themenheft

Topics Der in den *Topics* angegebene Wortschatz dient ausschließlich dem Verständnis der Texte bzw. als Hilfe für die Bewältigung von Aufgaben. Der im Textteil angegebene Wortschatz ist **nicht identisch** mit dem Lernvokabular auf der CD-ROM. Die Wörter sind in unterschiedlicher Weise aufbereitet:

Annotations Die *Annotations* dienen zur Erklärung nicht erschließbarer, für das Textverständnis zentraler Wörter und Begriffe. Sie stehen in der Randspalte und enthalten bei Bedarf auch die phonetische Umschrift.

Word bank Unter dem Titel *Word bank* erhalten die S eine Zusammenstellung von auf das Thema bezogenen Wörtern – bekannten und neuen – zur sprachlichen Bewältigung der Diskussions- oder Kommentierungsaufgaben. Die roten Kästchen stehen unmittelbar bei den Aufgaben.

Vocabulary sheets auf der CD-ROM

CD-ROM Die Organisation des Wortschatzes geschieht mit Hilfe der *Vocabulary sheets* auf der CD-ROM. Das Schülerheft bzw. Themenheft enthält lediglich zwei Seiten als Muster mit Erläuterungen

(Seite 58/59). Das Themenheft bietet eine dreispaltige Vorlage zur Gestaltung der *Vocabulary sheets* an:

Gestaltung Die linke Spalte ist für die zu erlernende Vokabel bestimmt (Einzelwort oder Wendung). Die mittlere Spalte kann Antonyme, Synonyme, Bezüge zur Wortfamilie usw. enthalten. Bei Einzelwörtern in der linken Spalte bietet sie vor allem wichtige Kollokationen. Die rechte Spalte ist für die deutsche Übersetzung der Lernvokabel und wichtiger Kollokationen vorgesehen.

Editierbar Die *Vocabulary sheets* werden für die S in einer Version mit Lücken angeboten. In der Regel ist nur die linke Spalte gefüllt und damit der zu lernende Wortschatz definiert. Es ist die Aufgabe der S, die leeren Spalten im Rahmen der Textarbeit zu füllen. Auf diese Weise erarbeiten sie sich den chronologischen Wortschatz weitgehend selbstständig. Der Inhalt der mittleren und rechten Spalte wird nur punktuell vorgegeben, um Variationsmöglichkeiten zu eröffnen und den S immer wieder Hinweise auf Vernetzungstechniken für die Wortschatzarbeit zu geben. Durch die Editierbarkeit der Word-Dokumente haben die S die Gelegenheit, jederzeit nach Wunsch weiteres Vokabular hinzuzufügen.

Online-Link 601016-0001 Für L steht das komplett ausgefüllte Vokabular zusätzlich online bei www.klett.de zur Verfügung. Der Online-Link des Lehrerheftes lautet: 601016-0001. Auf diese Weise besteht die Möglichkeit, jederzeit Vokabeltests schreiben zu lassen und diese auf komfortable Weise korrigieren zu können.

Organisation der Wortschatzarbeit

Chronologisch Aus der Reihenfolge der Vokabeln in den Texten ergibt sich ein chronologischer textbezogener Aufbau des Lernwortschatzes. Insgesamt können die S auf diese Weise einen Lernwortschatz von ca. 400–500 Wörtern pro Themenheft aufbauen. Die CD-ROM bietet zusätzlich *Vocabulary sheets* zu bestimmten Themengebieten an. In diesen Listen sind die wichtigsten Vokabeln pro Themengebiet enthalten. Ein Großteil dieser Vokabeln ergibt sich aus den Texten und ist bereits im chronologischen Wortschatz zu finden. Wichtiger, noch fehlender Wortschatz wird

Thematisch ergänzt, sodass die S am Ende thematisch gruppierte Lernwortlisten vorliegen haben, die es ihnen ermöglichen, sich optimal auf die mündliche oder schriftliche Textproduktion zu einem bestimmten Thema vorzubereiten. Der Inhalt der Wortlisten zu bestimmten Texten oder Themen kann von L als verbindlich erklärt und ggf. in Vokabeltests überprüft werden. L und S können somit unabhängig voneinander entscheiden, ob sie nur mit den chronologischen oder auch mit den thematischen Wortlisten arbeiten möchten.

Topics im Themenheft

Topics Das Themenheft *India* enthält vier *Topics:*
Topic 1: A plural country
Topic 2: The wounds of history
Topic 3: Different worlds
Topic 4: East meets West

Tasks Die *Topics* bieten ein vielseitiges und abwechslungsreiches Übungsangebot mit dem Ziel, die S zu einer textsortengerechten Produktion von gesprochener und geschriebener Sprache zu befähigen. Dabei stehen die Anforderungen der Abiturprüfung selbst und die Bewältigung der verschiedenen Lern- und Arbeitsbereiche der Oberstufe im Mittelpunkt. Grundsätzlich orientiert sich das Übungsangebot an den Anforderungsbereichen *Comprehension, Analysis*

Operatoren und *Evaluation* sowie an der Erarbeitung der jeweiligen Operatoren. Darüber hinaus ermöglicht die Übungsfolge in dem Themenheft *India* einen lebendigen und motivierenden Unterricht.

Kompetenzen Neben den textanalytischen Fragestellungen spielen auch Aufgaben zu den Kompetenzen eine wichtige Rolle. Dies sind u. a. *Discussing, Debating*, Recherche (auch über Online-Links), Präsentation, Projekte, *Creative writing*, Wortschatzaufbau, *Mediation*, Hörverstehen, Hör-/Sehverstehen, Ergebnissicherung. Die Übungen sind für die unterschiedlichsten

Sozialformen Sozialformen konzipiert. Häufig wird Gruppen- oder Partnerarbeit empfohlen. Durch die sinnvolle Kombination der verschiedenen Aufgaben entsteht so ein anregendes Übungsangebot, das die zielgerichtete Vorbereitung auf die Abiturprüfung gewährleistet, gleichzeitig aber die immer wiederkehrende Umwälzung durch nur wenige gleichförmige Übungsformate verhindert. Das Übungsangebot im Themenheft *India* orientiert sich damit auch an der Verwendung der englischen Sprache über das Abitur hinaus.

Servicematerial im Anhang

Projects Das Themenheft *India* enthält im Anhang (Seite 50–57) vier Projektvorschläge:
Project 1: A cultural trip to India
Project 2: A literary contest
Project 3: Myths and legends
Project 4: A taste of India
Die *Projects* sind in mehrere *Steps* untergliedert. Die S erhalten Hinweise zur Umsetzung (*How to give a multimedia presentation, How to present a literary analysis, How to plan and write an expository paper, How to present an archetypal film, How to create a successful display*) sowie nützliche Wendungen in *Word banks* (*Expressions for holiday bookings, Talking about writers and novels: 10 strategies with useful phrases, Food preparation*).

Worksheets Nach den *Projects* bietet das Themenheft Informationen zur Konzeption der Wortschatzarbeit (Seite 58/59). Hier wird die Organisation der *Vocabulary sheets* erläutert und die S finden Muster einer textbezogenen chronologischen und einer thematischen Wortschatzseite mit Hinweisen zur Verwendung:

- *How to work with the text-based vocabulary files*
- *How to work with the thematic vocabulary files*

Revision files Zu den vier *Topics* werden vier methodisch jeweils modifizierte *Revision files* angeboten (Seite 60–63), in die die S die wichtigsten Daten und Informationen eintragen können. Die *Revision files* sind ein Instrument zur Ergebnissicherung und zur Wiederholung. Sie können gezielt zur Klausur- oder Prüfungsvorbereitung eingesetzt werden. Ein Erwartungshorizont befindet sich hier im Lehrerheft im Anhang (Seite 109–112).

Methodenhefte

Methodenhefte Das Themenheft *India* kann ideal ergänzt werden durch eine Auswahl aus den ebenfalls im „Abi Workshop Englisch" zur Verfügung stehenden Methodenheften. Je nach den Notwendigkeiten der Lerngruppe können gezielt Defizite aufgearbeitet oder besondere Schwerpunkte gesetzt werden. Auch die individuelle Förderung von S ist möglich. Alle Methodenhefte sind konsequent auf die Anforderungen der Oberstufe und des Abiturs ausgerichtet. Sie sind sowohl für den Klassenunterricht als auch für das Selbststudium geeignet. Die jeweils beiliegende CD-ROM enthält alle Lösungen und Erwartungshorizonte.

Lehrerheft

Lehrerheft Das Lehrerheft setzt sich zum Ziel, einen wirksamen Beitrag zu einer effektiven und zeitsparenden Unterrichtsvorbereitung und -durchführung zu leisten. Die folgenden Elemente dienen in besonderer Weise zur Arbeitserleichterung:

Didaktisches Inhaltsverzeichnis Eine Erstinformation über die Inhalte der *Topics* bietet ein didaktisches Inhaltsverzeichnis, das in knapper und übersichtlicher Form über Textsorte/Thema, Unterrichtsmethoden, *Input boxes*, Kompetenzen und Textproduktion informiert. Hier sind außerdem die Textlängen (Wortanzahl) und Erscheinungsjahre der Originaltexte verzeichnet.

Unterrichtsverlauf Es folgen Hinweise zum Unterrichtsverlauf, einschließlich der Hintergrundinformationen, methodischen Schritte, dem Lernvokabular, aller Unterrichtsergebnisse, Querverweise,

Ergebnissicherung Alternativen, Hausaufgaben, Zusatzmaterialien usw. Die methodisch-didaktischen Erläuterungen werden zugunsten einer knappen, übersichtlichen Benutzerführung z.T. stichwortartig angeboten. Besonderer Wert wurde auf die Sicherung der Unterrichtsergebnisse in Form von Lösungsvorschlägen gelegt. Bei zahlreichen Texten und Übungen gibt es ausführlichere Vorschläge, insbesondere dann, wenn die Unterrichtsergebnisse für die Klausur- und Prüfungsvorbereitung relevant sind und sich auf elementare oder für die S schwierige Lernbereiche erstrecken (z.B. bei den Form-Inhalt-Beziehungen). Die S erhalten so die Chance, ihr Wissen und ihre Methodenkompetenz systematisch aufzubauen, das Gelernte zu vernetzen und – vor allem – noch einmal nachzuschauen, wenn sie etwas vergessen haben.

Servicematerial im Anhang

Sequenzplaner Im Anhang des Lehrerhefts befinden sich weitere nützliche Materialien für die Unterrichtsplanung. Den Auftakt bildet ein Sequenzplaner (Seite 73/74), der in knapper und übersichtlicher Form Aufschluss über die Kernsequenzen und die Vertiefungsmaterialien gibt. Damit wird die Zuordnung der Texte für Grund- und Leistungskurse auf einen Blick deutlich.

Kopiervorlagen Es folgen zu jedem der vier *Topics* weiterführende Arbeitsblätter als Kopiervorlagen (Seite 75–87). Die Kopiervorlagen (KVs) vertiefen die behandelten Themen und dienen entweder zur Festigung des Lernwortschatzes oder zur inhaltlichen Erweiterung der Themenbereiche.

Lösungen Die Lösungen (Seite 88–90) stehen ebenfalls als Kopiervorlage zur Verfügung. Sie können den S zur Selbstkontrolle ausgehändigt werden.

Klausurvorschläge Neben den Kopiervorlagen befindet sich im Anhang zu jedem *Topic* ein Klausurvorschlag (Seite 91–101). Die vier Klausurvorschläge decken unterschiedliche Textsorten ab, z.B. Sachtexte, Romanauszug und Rezension. Der notwendige Wortschatz wird unter dem Text als *Annotations* angeboten, darauf folgt eine Auswahl an abwechslungsreichen *Tasks*.

Erwartungshorizont Zu den vier Klausurvorschlägen gibt es für die Hand der L einen Erwartungshorizont (Seite 102–108). Neben den Lösungsvorschlägen zu den *Tasks* befinden sich hier die nötigen Textinformationen und Quellenangaben.

Revision files Den Abschluss des Serviceteils im Lehrerbuch bildet der Erwartungshorizont zu den *Revision files* (Seite 109–112).

Topic 1: A plural country

pp. 4–13

Didaktisches Inhaltsverzeichnis

Bearbeitungszeitraum: 8–12 Unterrichtsstunden

Textsorte / Thema	Unterrichts-methoden	*Input boxes*	Kompetenzen	Textproduktion
Some quotes about India (195 words)				SB, Seite 4/5, LB, Seite 7–9
Combination of visuals, quotes, map/First information on India	Kursgespräch Gruppenarbeit Online-Link: 601006-0001 Zusatzmaterial: Kopiervorlage 1, Kopiervorlage 2		Orientierungswissen Bildbeschreibung/-analyse Sehverstehen Leseverstehen Gespräche führen	*Describing and assessing pictures* *Analysing quotations* *Brainstorming for keywords* *Comparing pictures* *Summarising aspects*
Indian identity is forged in diversity, 2007 (1037 words)				SB, Seite 6/7, LB, Seite 9–11
Newspaper article/ Indian national identity	Kursgespräch Partnerarbeit Online-Link: 601006-0002 Zusatzmaterial: Kopiervorlage 3	*Tip: Indian states* *Fact file: Languages and dialects in India* *Word bank*	Leseverstehen Gespräche führen	*Making a mind map* *Scanning a text* *Analysing stylistic devices* *Outlining ideas on German identity*
[1◎] **A visit to the Cow Product Research Centre, 2006** (862 words)				SB, Seite 8/9, LB, Seite 12–15
Book excerpt/The role of the sacred cow in Hinduism	*Transcript* (539 words) Kursgespräch Partnerarbeit Online-Link: 601006-0003	*Fact file: Religion in India* *Word bank: Talking about how to react to other cultures*	Leseverstehen Gespräche führen Argumentieren Hörverstehen Mediation	*Analysing an attitude* *Discussing views* *Acting as an interpreter*
[1🎬] **Hindu gods** (222 words)				SB, Seite 10, LB, Seite 15/16
Factual information, video clip/Hinduism	Kursgespräch Online-Link: 601006-0004	*Fact file: Hindu gods* *Word banks*	Orientierungswissen Hör-/Sehverstehen Gespräche führen Recherchieren	*Taking notes*
What Happened to the Elephant? (226 words)				SB, Seite 11, LB, Seite 16/17
Poem/Hindu Gods Ganesha and Shiva	Kursgespräch Partnerarbeit	*VIP file: Sujata Bhatt*	Leseverstehen Gespräche führen Argumentieren Recherchieren	*Identifying a viewpoint* *Analysing structure and content* *Examining poetic devices* *Giving a presentation*
A visual dialect, 1998 (974 words)				SB, Seite 12/13, LB, Seite 17–19
Novel excerpt/Living between the castes	Kursgespräch Online-Link: 601006-0005 Zusatzmaterial: Klausurvorschlag 1	*Fact file: Rajasthan* *Fact file: The history of the caste system in India*	Leseverstehen Gespräche führen Argumentieren	*Collecting examples* *Commenting on an idea*

Unterrichtsverlauf

Magazine covers/ Quotes/Map

Lead-in: Some quotes about India pp. 4–5

HINTERGRUNDINFO

Basic information

Geography: *India borders on China in the northeast. Other neighbours are Pakistan to the west, Nepal and Bhutan to the north, and Myanmar and Bangladesh to the east. In the southeast India fronts the Bay of Bengal, in the southwest it fronts the Arabian Sea.*

The ***capital*** *of India is New Delhi (inhabitants 2008: metro area: 15,334,000, city proper: 9,817,439). India's largest cities are Mumbai (Bombay) (metro area: 18,336,000, city proper: 11,914,398), Kolkata (Calcutta) (metro area: 14,299,000, city proper: 4,760,800) and Bangalore (4,461,100 inhabitants).*

India comprises an ***area*** *of 3,166,414 square km and can be divided into three major geographic regions: the Himalayas, along its northern border, the Indo-Gangetic Plain and the southern and central region. India's three great river systems – the Ganges, the Indus, and the Brahmaputra – have extensive deltas and all rise in the Himalayas.*

India's ***population*** *is estimated at 1,147,996 million (2008).*

Languages: *Hindi, English (both official), and other Indo-European languages, including Bengali, Kashmiri, Marathi, and Urdu; Dravidian languages; hundreds from several other language families.*

Religions: *Hinduism; also Islam, Christianity, Sikhism, Buddhism, Jainism, Zoroastrianism.*

Currency: *rupee*

System of government: *India is a federal republic with two legislative houses; its chief of state is the president, and the head of government is the prime minister.*

Note: *The map in the pupil's book is simplified, as it neglects the fact that e.g. Myanmar (formerly Burma) also belonged to the British Indian Empire at various times. It shows India shortly before Partition.*

Lernwortschatz *mortal, to adhere to, to inhabit, to possess, to embody, to be stunned, lush, exotic, to render, fervent, to stride, entrepreneurial, to embrace, diversity, passionate*

Materialien → **Online-Link: 601006-0001**

Die Auftaktseiten bieten ein buntes Bild für den Einstieg der S in die neue Thematik. Bevor mit dem Bild-, Text- und Kartenmaterial gearbeitet wird, sollten die S zunächst ihre Assoziationen zu Indien in einer Stichwortliste zusammenstellen. Diese Liste können die S selbstständig mit dem in den Texten und Materialien gewonnenen Hintergrundwissen ergänzen.

Brainstorming

1 [ååå] *What do you associate with India?*

Zusatzmaterial → **Kopiervorlage 1 (Quiz on India) • Kopiervorlage 2 (Map of India)**

Lösungsvorschlag ***Keywords***

- *tradition*
- *former British colony, English as official language*
- *Mahatma Gandhi, struggle for independence*
- *caste system*
- *Hinduism, Islam, Buddhism and other religions*
- *conflict with Pakistan*
- *huge population, social contrasts*
- *information technology*

Erweiterung

- **Kopiervorlage 1** (Seite 75) enthält elf Fragen zu Indiens Geografie, Geschichte und Religion sowie zu bekannten Persönlichkeiten des Landes. Mit Hilfe dieses Quizzes testen die S ihr Vorwissen zum indischen Subkontinent.
- **Kopiervorlage 2** (Seite 76) bietet eine Landkarte, die die S zur Bearbeitung des Quizzes mit heranziehen können.

Discussion

2 *Look at the woman in the yellow sari. Imagine who she might be, …*

Aufgabe **a)** eignet sich auch als Partnerarbeit, Aufgabe **b)** für eine Diskussion im Plenum.

Lösungsvorschlag

a)
- *The woman might be an elderly Hindi woman who has lived all her life in a rural area on the Ganges.*
- *She might be the mother of four children and grandmother to a considerable number of grandchildren who has struggled hard to make ends meet.*
- *She might have felt a light breeze on her skin when she was standing on the river bank and was looking at the water, recalling some important stages in her life and musing on her experiences.*
- *She might be convinced that India is the best place in the world to be born right now because the country offers possibilities to the young generation that the elderly could only have dreamed of; the traditional caste system has lost its overall influence on society and thus personal achievement enables the young to reach beyond the traditional role that their parents or grandparents might have been reduced to.*

b) Individuelle S-Beiträge.

Analysis

3 *Examine and compare the three covers.*

Lösungsvorschlag

The cover of the Guardian depicts a bare-footed woman in a sari who is quoted with the words "This is the best place in the world to be born right now." The quote and the additional information on the focus of the special newspaper issue, "The new India", is clearly visible against the background of the bright yellow colour of the sari. The picture only shows the back of the woman, so the reader is invited to speculate on who she might be and why she might have said this about India. The words "The new India" imply that the country has fundamentally changed and is on the brink of a completely new development. This is in stark contrast to the traditional clothing of the woman who is standing on a pebbled river bank.

The photograph in the middle is the cover of a Time magazine issue which focuses on India's role as the next economic superpower and its impact on the United States. Against the background of a traditional pattern in bright yellow and orange, is a portrait of a young Indian woman wearing traditional pearl jewellery. The bindi, i.e. the ornamental mark on the forehead between her two eyebrows, indicates that the woman values the Hindu tradition. This impression is somewhat in contrast to the headset the woman is wearing. It might be a hint that she works for a call centre or the like. The words "India Inc." attract the reader's attention, too, due to the size of the letters and the implication that the whole Indian subcontinent is a huge corporation.

On the third cover, another one from Time magazine, India is symbolically represented by a traditionally painted and adorned elephant. The depiction of the elephant chosen for the special report on India's 60th anniversary of independence illustrates the central statement printed below the headline of the front page: "India Charges Ahead" – "It faces challenges the size of an elephant …". The choice of words demonstrates that India is rushing forward and thus "is living up to the dream of 1947". The elephant was caught in motion and so the picture underlines the two aspects of the statement in an effective way.

Comprehension

4 *Read the quotations by people who travelled India …*

Aufgabe **a)** eignet sich für eine schriftliche **Hausaufgabe**. Sie kann alternativ aber auch nach einer Stillarbeitsphase in der Klasse besprochen werden.

Lösungsvorschlag

a) ***Main aspect:*** *people. The Greek traveller* ***Apollonius Tyaneus*** *points out that the Indian people live in this country without actually sticking to it; that they inhabit the cities without being attached to them and that they own everything without actually being dependent on these things.*

Main aspect: *wisdom (language, philosophy, religion, science, politics). The philosopher and historian* ***William James Durant*** *points to the fact that India is the origin not only of the European people and languages but also of our philosophy, mathematics and the ideals that are promoted by Christianity as well as of our system of self-government and democracy.*

Main aspect: *sensual experience.* ***Keith Bellows*** *was fascinated by the brightness and intensity of colours, smells, tastes, and sounds which differed very much from everything he had experienced so far and which fundamentally changed his outlook on life. He also admired the richness, the beauty and the exotic architecture of the country.*

Main aspect: *change, contradictions. The extract from the* ***Lonely Planet Guide*** *refers to the deeply-rooted traditions, but also points to the rising importance of information technology for India's economy and sums up that India "embraces diversity passionately" and thus differs from most other countries in the world.*

b) Individuelle S-Beiträge.

Newspaper article

Indian identity is forged in diversity pp. 6–7

HINTERGRUNDINFO

Languages in India: *There are more than 1,600 languages and dialects spoken in India. As defined in the Constitution of India, the official language of the Republic of India is Hindi. According to the 2001 Indian Census native speakers of Hindi dialects account for 41% of the Indian population. English, which serves as a lingua franca, is a secondary official language at the federal level. Apart from English, the Indian constitution contains a list of 22 scheduled languages. According to the official language resolution of 1968, "it is necessary in the interest of the educational and cultural advancement of the country that concerted measures should be taken for the full development of these languages". The individual Indian states specify their own official language(s) through legislation. As many as 35 languages are spoken by more than a million native speakers, 122 by more than 10,000. The twelve most important languages are Hindi (spoken by more than 420 million speakers), Bengali (approximately 83 million speakers), Telugu (ca. 74 million), Marathi (ca. 72 million), Tamil (ca. 61 million), Urdu (ca. 52 million), Gujarati, Kannada, Malayalam, Oriya, Punjabi and Assamese (ca. 13 million).*

Lernwortschatz *to require, inconceivable, startling, affirmation, pluralism, archetypal, to cherish sb/sth, to adhere to sth, to mingle, to throng, caste, notion, distinguishable, apparent, commonality, to accommodate sth, compatriot, secular, partition, eligible, to emerge (from), ancient, to sustain, to impose sth upon sb, sumptuous, to complement, to endure, creed, conviction, to accustom sb to sth, complexion, to absorb*

Materialien → **Online-Link: 601006-0002**

Der Text wird zunächst im Plenum gelesen oder von den S bereits zu Hause vorbereitend erarbeitet. Hinweis auf den Tipp und die *Fact file* zu *Languages and dialects in India.*

Brainteaser

1 *Collect ideas about what you think helps to create a feeling of ...*

L kann bei Bedarf die folgenden Hinweise zur Bearbeitung dieser Aufgabenstellung geben:
A feeling of national identity among the citizens of a nation might be created by

- *a shared history*
- *a common language*
- *the same ethnic origin and shared descent*
- *shared customs and traditions*
- *religious ties*
- *etc.*

Lösungsvorschlag Individuelle S-Beiträge.

Comprehension

2 *Develop a mind map around the concept of 'Indian diversity'.*

Aufgabe **a)** eignet sich für eine Stillarbeitsphase. Aufgabe **b)** bildet die Grundlage für eine Diskussion im Plenum. Hinweis auf die Worthilfen in der *Word bank*.

Lösungsvorschlag

a) ***Mind map***

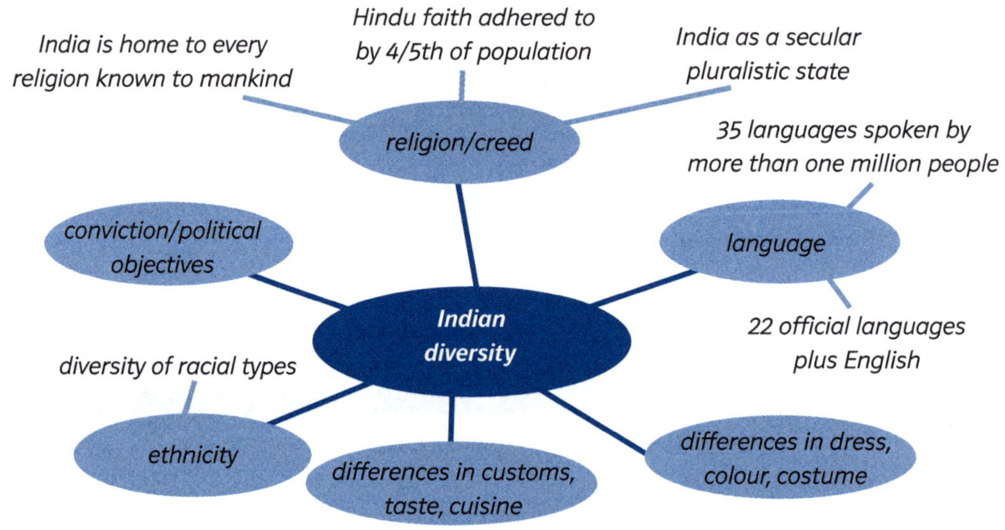

→ ***India:*** *one land embracing many; unity in diversity is accomplished by the strong belief in the principles of democracy*

b) ***Evaluation***

Almost all the ideas collected for task 1 are not really adequate to define Indian national identity. Indians do share a common history, of course, but because of their various ethnic origins and races (ll. 41 ff.) they do not share the same descent. Thus, Indians have a huge variety of customs and traditions, convictions, tastes, appearances etc. (ll. 64 ff.). Neither does a common language provide the basis of a national identity. According to the fact file, there are more than 1,600 languages and dialects spoken in India. The country also comprises a vast amount of different religions and creeds, thus being "a secular pluralist state that is home to every religion known to mankind" (ll. 45 ff.). So national identity is not a result of shared religious ties, either. In fact, the only appropriate category thought about in task 1, a shared history, can serve as a basis to define Indian national identity. As the author points out, "Indian nationalism has therefore always been the nationalism of an idea. It is the idea of an ever-ever land – emerging from an ancient civilisation, united by a shared history, sustained by a pluralist democracy." (ll. 50 ff.) This implies that India's national identity is based on the knowledge that the country looks back on thousands of years of civilisation and that it prides itself on its system of government, a pluralistic democracy. Rather than being the result of common things, of shared elements, Indian national identity is constituted by "unity in diversity" (l. 69), as India is "one land embracing many" (l. 63) and thus defies any traditional definitions of national identity.

Analysis

3 *Scan the text for references to the principles of government in India.*

Aufgabe **a)** eignet sich auch als Partnerarbeit, Aufgabe **b)** kann gemeinsam im gelenkten Unterrichtsgespräch erarbeitet werden.

Lösungsvorschlag

a) *The text mentions that India is a pluralist democracy (l. 53) with a prime minister as a political leader (ll. 2–5; ll. 76 ff). India has a written constitution, which, for example, recognises 22 official languages (ll. 40 ff.). According to the author, India's democracy does not restrict people or force them to adapt to some majority conviction (l. 54). Despite all the differences Indians share the belief that "in a democracy you don't really need to agree – except on the ground rules of how you will disagree." (ll. 66 ff.)*

b) ***Concept of the Indian nation:*** *The author stresses that India as a nation is not based on a common language, ethnicity, religion, geography or territory (ll. 40–50). Indian nationalism, he* *points out, has always been "the nationalism of an idea" (l. 51). Its core concept focuses on the ideas of diversity and pluralism (l. 53, l. 55), which maintain India's differences. Thus the Indian nation emerges as "one land embracing many" (l. 63).*

Stylistic devices
- ***anaphora** (ll. 40–48): The phrase "Not + noun, since …" is repeated five times at the beginning of successive sentences. The author uses this stylistic device to highlight that traditional concepts of nationality do not apply to the Indian national identity.*
- ***neologism** (l. 52): The author points out that Indian nationalism is "the idea of an ever-ever land", which is a word created in analogy to never-never land, an imaginary dream world. Thus the writer emphasises that the concept of Indian national identity is not an unrealistic notion but is based on ancient traditions and a common history as well as the firm belief in pluralist democracy (ll. 52 ff.), an idea which is also highlighted by a climax (ll. 52–54): The series of words "emerging …, united …, sustained" underline the author's argumentation.*
- ***paradox** (ll. 54–55): The statement "The whole point of Indian pluralism is you can be many things and one thing" seems to be self-contradictory or opposed to common sense. On closer examination, however, it illustrates the author's opinion that no matter whether you are a "good Muslim" or "a good Keralite", you can also be "a good Indian all at once" (l. 56), a concept which is further underlined by the parallelism "a good Muslim, a good Keralite and a good Indian" (ll. 55–56).*
- ***extended metaphor** (ll. 59–62): The author says that "India is a thali, a selection of sumptuous dishes in different bowls." Thus the author compares the Indian population to the different dishes which are important parts of a good meal, although they may be completely different and do "not necessarily mix with the next" (l. 60). Similarly the different groups in Indian society are all part of the whole, and although they might be entirely dissimilar, they comprise the Indian nation and form the Indian pluralist society.*
- ***alliteration** (ll. 64–65): The author employs a sentence comprising nine nouns beginning with the letter "c". He illustrates his notion that despite all the "differences of caste, creed, colour, conviction, culture, cuisine, costume and custom" a "consensus" is possible, thus confirming India's slogan "unity in diversity" (l. 69).*

Comment on the author's attitude: Individuelle S-Antworten.

Analysis **4 [👥] *Write a text outlining your ideas about German identity …***

Zusatzmaterial → **Kopiervorlage 3 (Working with words)**

Die S erledigen diese Aufgabe als schriftliche **Hausaufgabe**. Im Unterricht tauschen sie ihre Texte mit dem Nachbarn und besprechen Inhalt und Sprache der jeweiligen Texte.

Lösungsvorschlag ***Possible aspects students might include in their texts***
- *In the age of globalisation a definition of German identity has become difficult.*
- *German identity might be formed by the following aspects:*
  - *a common language*
  - *a core territory, particularly after German reunification in 1990*
  - *a shared religion (Christianity) for the majority of Germans*
  - *a strong belief in a pluralist democracy and a social market economy*
  - *a long tradition of shared customs and core values*
- *However, number of immigrants is rising – thus many people living in Germany come from completely different backgrounds and need to be integrated.*
- *Eastern Germans and Western Germans have been socialised in different ways: both have shaped German national identity.*
- *Germany's history (Third Reich) makes it difficult for Germans to openly show patriotism.*
- *Many young people say that they do no longer consider themselves as Germans but as Europeans.*

Erweiterung **Kopiervorlage 3** (Seite 77) bietet Übungen zur Vertiefung des Lernwortschatzes.

Book excerpt **A visit to the Cow Product Research Centre** pp. 8–9

HINTERGRUNDINFO

Religion in India: *In India religious beliefs and practices have a large impact on the personal lives of most inhabitants and influence daily public life. Religion is not only one of the most important facets of contemporary Indian life, it also shaped India's history, as the ancient culture of South Asia has predominantly been spread by religious texts. Religious thought and symbolism are the underlying foundations of much of the artistic heritage of the Indian subcontinent. A number of world religions originated in India, and others that started elsewhere found fertile ground for growth there. Approximately 80.5 % of the Indian population are devotees of* ***Hinduism****. From the early 8th century, Islam spread from the West throughout South Asia, to become the largest minority religion in India. In fact, with roughly 13.4 % of the population, the number of* ***Muslims*** *living in India is still almost equal to that of Muslims living in Pakistan.* ***Sikhism****, which started in Punjab in the 16th century, has spread throughout India and the world since the mid-19th century. Sikhs represent roughly two percent of India's population.* ***Buddhism*** *and* ***Jainism****, which both had a major influence on Indian art, philosophy, and society, remain important minority religions in India today.* ***Judaism*** *and* ***Zoroastrianism****, arriving originally with traders and exiles from the West, are represented by small populations, mostly concentrated on India's west coast. About 2.3 % of Indians are* ***Christians****.*

There is also a variety of independent ***tribal religious groups*** *in India, contributing to the remarkable diversity in Indian religious life. This diversity is enhanced by the fact that the complex doctrines and institutions of the great traditions, preserved through written documents, are divided into numerous schools of thought, sects, and paths of devotion. Furthermore, urbanisation and modernisation have resulted in the emergence of new religions, revivals, and reforms within the great traditions. In the countryside religious traditions constantly change, too, due to the fact that entire social groups – each with their own vision of the divine, are integrated. Thus ritual forms and mythology differ widely throughout the Indian subcontinent. Despite rising fundamentalism, however, Indian religions have demonstrated for many centuries a considerable degree of tolerance for alternative forms of worship. Since independence the Indian state has defined itself as a secular state. The government has officially declared itself separate from any religion. All forms of belief are granted equal status before the law. In practice this strict division between religion and state has been difficult to accomplish, however. Thus in states where the majority of the population embraces one religion, there is a danger of government politics being influenced by religious ideas.*

The role of the sacred cow in Hinduism: *In Hinduism, the cow is revered as the symbol of life and is associated with motherhood and Mother Earth as her products nurture the population. In early Hinduism, cows became animals which had to be protected. As cows have also been associated with different gods and identified early on with the Brahman or priestly class, killing a cow was considered equal to killing a Brahman. In many princely states where the monarch was Hindu, legislation against killing cows persisted into the 20th century. Hindus today do not eat beef. The role of the cow as a sacred animal can be traced back to the 7th century BC when the Indo-European peoples, pastoralists who moved from place to place to find water and food for their animals, entered India. As the cows were very valuable to them, these animals were assigned a special role in their religion. Slaughtering milk-producing cows was increasingly forbidden. Reverence for cows can be found throughout the religion's major texts and the five products of the cow – milk, curd (a thick soft substance that is formed when milk turns sour), butter, urine, and dung have been and are still being used in rites of healing, purification, and penance. In honour of their exalted status, cows often roam free in many Indian cities. Cow-friendly policies, however, have resulted in major difficulties. Approximately 40,000 cows live in New Delhi, for example. Thus cows living on rubbish in the streets or dangerously snarling traffic are a familiar sight to many Indians. Once a year, however, the cow as a sacred animal is particularly honoured. On Gopastami, "Cow Holiday", cows are washed and decorated in the temple and given offerings in the hope that their gifts of life will persist.*

Lernwortschatz *to seek to do sth, sacred, dung, tribal, to approach, vast, puddle, to tease sb, donation, gingerly, breed, indigenous, to wheel, to dangle, fierce, to recoil, unfazed, to bubble, obesity, to purify, to conceal, dandruff, to submit, application, utterly, to fertilise, to enrich, to emit, odour, merit, pile*

Materialien → **Online-Link: 601006-0003**

Der Text wird zunächst einmal im Plenum gelesen oder er wird von den S bereits zu Hause erarbeitet. Hinweis auf die *Fact file* zu *Religion in India.*

Comprehension

1 *On the basis of the text above, say how you would respond …*

Lösungsvorschlag

If I was invited to visit the Cow Product Research Centre I would happily accept the invitation and be pleased about the opportunity of getting an insight into the role of the sacred cow in Hinduism. I would point out that in Germany cows are primarily bred to provide meat and that I was amazed at the variety of products the research centre manufactured from this animal.

Or:

Assuming that I know the details the author reveals on The Cow Product Research Centre, I would try to politely decline the invitation. I would respond that I was aware that the institution offered an interesting insight into the role of the sacred cow in Hinduism. However, I would also point out that I could not walk around the place barefoot because I suffer from an allergy. Finally I would say that I really appreciate the invitation but that I do hope that they understand my wish to turn it down.

Analysis

2 *Analyse the writer's attitude to what he experienced and …*

Vorbereitung: Detailliertes Lesen in Einzelarbeit mit Notieren von relevanten Stellen und Kommentaren. Danach Austausch und wechselseitige Ergänzung in Partnerarbeit. Die Ergebnissicherung erfolgt im Kursgespräch.

Lösungsvorschlag

The author seems to relate his experiences at the Cow Product Research Centre with a smile. He obviously has ambiguous feelings towards the work of the institution. On the one hand, he seems to be revolted by some of the details he gets to see (e.g. the huge testicles of the bull or the smell from the dozens of cow urine bottles) and he appears not to be very convinced of the advantages of some products (cf. 37 ff). On the other hand, he is obviously quite impressed by the high scientific standard of the institution (l. 5) and acknowledges some "impressive uses for cow's product" (ll. 49–50).

On the whole, the author conveys his experiences in a slightly ironic tone and refers to most of the details in a humorous way. Throughout the text the author contrasts his own thoughts, feelings and observations with the comments of Mr Mansinghka, a senior activist of the World Council of Hinduism, who shows him around the research centre. The author does not comment on what his guide says but the readers will notice the slight ironic undertone and understand the author's attempt to question or mildly poke fun at what Mr Mansinghka points out (e.g. ll. 21 ff., ll. 40 ff., ll. 57 ff.). Only in one case does Edward Luce add one sentence which makes the whole situation even funnier: "'Now you are praying to the cow. She is my mother. She is your mother,' said Mansinghka. Mother seemed unfazed by all the attention" (ll. 27–28).

By employing various passive constructions or verbs indicating that he is not taking an active role, the author Edward Luce points out that he was somehow shoved into the cow shelter ("He wheeled me …", l. 18; "I was pushed …", l. 22; "I was somehow manoeuvred …", l. 23; "I was handed …", l. 24; "I had to circle …", l. 25) where he is forced to do certain tasks. Despite Mr Mansinghka's serious attempts to convince him of "the merits of the holy cow's products" (l. 56), the author seems to remain doubtful. The humorous way the author recalls the urine-derivative products and cow dung products, respectively, underlines his skepticism of the benefits of these products (ll. 36–38). In the next paragraph, however, Edward Luce becomes more serious. He considers Mansinghka's beliefs as "textbook fundamentalism" (l. 45) and illustrates his view by the enumeration "God made the world in six days; Eve was formed from Adam's rib; Ram was born on this precise spot; and so on" (l. 49). In the last paragraph of the text the author points out the stark contrast between the highly esteemed cows at the Cow Product Research Centre (ll. 57 ff.) and a cow in the streets of Nagpur, "with its head stuck in a large pile of rubbish, chewing through plastic" (ll. 60 ff.). As this was an everyday scene, "nobody seemed to mind" (l. 62).

Evaluation

3 [👥] *Using the impression you get of the writer's behaviour ...*

Diskussion über beide Teilaufgaben **a)** und **b)** in Kleingruppen. Hinweis auf die *Word bank* zu *Talking about how to react to other cultures.*

Lösungsvorschlag

a) *Although the author seems to be slightly revolted by and skeptical about some aspects of his experiences at the research centre, he remains compliant and polite. He seems to be rather tolerant and open-minded and acts accordingly even in some situations which seem to be quite awkward or even unpleasant for him. Discussion on what is or is not the appropriate way to react to unfamiliar customs or ways of thinking while in a foreign country:*

Appropriate
- *Keeping an open mind and trying to be tolerant as well as accepting the differences between one's own culture and the foreign one instead of being too critical and negative towards it at all times.*
- *Being flexible and willing to adapt one's lifestyle and thinking to the lifestyle and thinking in the foreign country.*
- *Showing respect for unfamiliar customs and traditions in a foreign country.*

Inappropriate
- *Causing offence by violating rules or conventions typical of that country or a certain religious faith (e.g. improper dressing in churches, temples, mosques, etc.).*
- *Unsettling people by insisting on preconceived ideas that you have on the country and/or the people there.*
- *Being too strict and firm and insisting on keeping up one's familiar lifestyle and notions.*
- *Acting disrespectfully towards foreigners in unfamiliar situations.*
- *Labelling cultural norms and values that are contrary to one's own as "false" or "dangerous".*

b) ***'Dangerous' topics in intercultural exchanges might be:***
- *The difficult past of a country (e.g. the persecution and murder of Jews by the Nazi regime in Germany or the Apartheid system in South Africa) as citizens of that country might feel they are being blamed for the actions of their ancestors.*
- *The role of women in a country in which equality between the sexes is not granted, as citizens of that country might feel misunderstood.*
- *Conflicts within a country (e.g. the difficult relationship between Israel and the Palestinians or the conflict around Tibet) as citizens of that country might feel that foreigners do not have enough information and insight to be able to neutrally consider the problem.*
- *Alleged or proven human rights violations in a country, as citizens of that country might think that this is a topic no other country should interfere with.*

Comprehension

4 [1◉] *Listening/Mediation: You are with a group of German tourists ...*

Materialien → **CD, Track 1**

[1◉] L präsentiert den Hörtext von der CD. Das *Transcript* steht als PDF ebenfalls auf der CD zur Verfügung. Hinweis auf die Wendungen in der *Word bank.*

Lösungsvorschlag

- *My friend is very sorry that she is not really able to understand you. May I help by trying to act as an interpreter? She would really love to talk to you. (...)*
- Er ist einverstanden, dass ich dolmetsche. Er sagte eben, dass er sehr glücklich darüber sei, Gäste aus Deutschland in Delhi zu sehen und er hofft, dass uns unser Aufenthalt hier gefällt. (...)
- *Our stay here is a terrific experience. This morning we had the chance to visit Akshardham. My friend was very much impressed by the huge temple complex. She has also learned a lot about your culture. (...)*
- Er findet auch, dass der Akshardham Tempelkomplex sehr schön ist. Er selbst allerdings ist kein Hindu, sondern Moslem. (...)
- *My friend would like to apologise and is concerned that she might have offended you.*

- Er sagt, dass diese fälschliche Annahme überhaupt kein Problem sei. Es ist ein sehr verständlicher Fehler, denn die große Mehrheit der indischen Bevölkerung sind Hindus. Er ist der Meinung, dass man, auch wenn jeder seine eigene Religion hat, die Schönheit der Tempel, Moscheen und so weiter der jeweils anderen Religion bewundern kann, auch wenn man selbst dort nicht betet. In einem Land, das so vielfältig ist wie Indien, ist es wichtig, tolerant zu sein. (…)
- *Thank you for being so understanding. In fact, my friend here has already noticed that people in India are very tolerant not only towards foreigners who might say something silly but also towards their fellow countrymen and -women. She became aware of that when we visited the government building and were informed about the political system. She admires the way democracy works in such a huge country." (…)*
- Um ehrlich zu sein, sagt er, ist es nicht immer leicht. Die Regierung ist immer eine Koalitionsregierung, denn obwohl es große nationale Parteien gibt, bekommen die vielen kleinen regionalen Parteien viele Stimmen. Daher sind die verschiedenen Parteien darauf angewiesen zusammenzuarbeiten. Aber zumindest bedeutet das auch, dass die Interessen unterschiedlicher Gruppierungen und Regionen in der Regel im Parlament repräsentiert werden. (…)
- *Do you mind if I ask where you come from? (…)*
- Er kommt aus dem Punjab. Er bleibt hier nur eine Nacht. Er hat in ein paar Minuten einen Geschäftstermin, so dass er jetzt leider gehen muss. Er würde das Gespräch aber sehr gerne fortsetzen, vielleicht diesen Abend, wenn es möglich wäre. (…)
- *My friend would have loved to continue the conversation but is very sorry that this won't be possible tonight. We are going out to listen to an Indian music performance. Thank you very much for the interesting conversation, and that you have been so patient and understanding. Good luck to you. (…)*
- Er hat sich sehr gefreut und wünscht uns das Allerbeste für den Rest unseres Aufenthalts in Indien.

Factual information/Poem

Hindu gods/What Happened to the Elephant? pp. 10–11

HINTERGRUNDINFO

***Sujata Bhatt** is an Indian poet who was born in Ahmedabad, India, in 1956. She grew up in Pune, India, and in the United States. She now lives in Bremen, Germany, with her husband and daughter. Sujata Bhatt has published six collections of poems. Her poems have been printed in various journals in the United Kingdom, Ireland, the United States, and Canada and in a variety of anthologies. Her work has been translated into more than 20 languages. Bhatt has been awarded, among others, the Commonwealth Poetry Prize (Asia) and the Cholmondeley Award. Many of her poems focus on love and violence as themes, and are occupied with such aspects as racism and cultural identity.*

multiplicity, to worship, deity, manifestation, to achieve, reincarnation, cycle, trinity, to preserve, to maintain, to surround, ornate;
curiosity, nosy, to probe, to prolong, to revive, to gaze, framed, to rot, carcass, crumpled, vulture, to sway, trunk

Materialien → **Online-Link: 601006-0004**

Als Einstieg lesen die S die *Fact file* zu *Hindu gods* in Stillarbeit.

Comprehension

1 [1] *First watch the video without writing anything down.*

Materialien → **Film 1 (India with Sanjeev Bhaskar – A visit to Kolkata)**

[1] Der Videoclip wird zunächst einmal vorgespielt, ohne dass die S Notizen anfertigen (Teilaufgabe **a**). Danach erhalten die S die Gelegenheit, sich im Plenum über ihre ersten Eindrücke auszutauschen. Vor dem zweiten Anschauen (Teilaufgabe **b**) verteilt L an drei S Folien, auf die diese ihre Ergebnisse zu *1. Kali, 2. The Ganges* und *3. Kali Puja* notieren. Die übrigen S schreiben

ihre Ergebnisse in ihr Heft und vergleichen anschließend ihre Notizen mit den von den drei ausgewählten S präsentierten Aspekten. Hinweis auf die *Word bank*.

Lösungsvorschlag **a)** ***Aspects students might mention***

- *The street scenes: man being shaven by a barber outdoors, children playing in dirty streets.*
- *The lush colours: e.g. the yellow flower ornaments at the beginning of the video; the displaying of gods and goddesses in the ceremony at the river Ganges, etc.*
- *The river Ganges: people washing their clothes in the water, the fact that the river is one of the most polluted ones in Asia, the fact that for the 800 million Hindus the river is the holiest one in the world.*
- *The ever present spirituality in this country.*
- *The ceremony of consigning the deities to the holy water of the Ganges: the rather chaotic scene at the river banks, the immersion itself, the noise, the music.*

b) **1. *Kali***

- *Kali, who has given the city its name, is Kolkata's patron goddess and is considered as the supreme ruler in this city.*
- *She occupies a special place in Hindu mythology: her followers believe that she controls the cosmic cycle in which the world continually destroys itself only to be reborn; in former times it was thought that the only way to appease Kali's wrath was with a human sacrifice, but today flowers will do.*

2. *The Ganges*

- *Entire lives are lived out at some stretches of the river.*
- *The Ganges delta is one of the most densely populated regions in the world.*
- *The Ganges is also one of the most contaminated rivers in Asia.*
- *For Hindus the river is much more than just a body of water: the Ganges is the holiest river on the planet. For them the water can wash away your sins, cure all ills and provide a gateway to the next world. It is itself divine.*
- *A newborn devout Hindu baby will be blessed with the Ganges water and that same devout Hindu at the end of his life will be immersed into this water after death in the form of ashes after cremation. To the Hindus of this country, none of these things contradict; all of those things are acceptable. It takes a place like India with its mass population and its drive towards spirituality and spiritual understanding to accept this river as all those things.*

3. *Kali Puja*

- *The ceremony takes place as evening falls.*
- *The temporary shrines that have sprung up all over the city are dismantled and the deities who have presided over them are consigned to the holy water of the Ganges.*
- *People bring their own deities down to immerse them in the river to remind the devotees that each day and each life cycle has an element of cleansing to it; so death is not the end, as there is a cleansing and then there is a rebirth.*
- *The Christian belief in "ashes to ashes, dust to dust" equals the Hindu belief that you basically come from the elements and you return to the elements.*

Analysis

2 *Read the poem on the opposite page. Identify …*

Hinweis auf die *VIP file* zu Sujata Bhatt. Das Gedicht wird im Plenum zweimal laut gelesen. Nach einer kurzen Partnerarbeitsphase erfolgt die gemeinsame Ergebnissicherung für Aufgabe **a)**. Aufgabe **b)** wird im Kursgespräch erarbeitet, Teilaufgabe **c)** eignet sich für eine Stillarbeitsphase oder als schriftliche **Hausaufgabe**, Aufgabe **d)** wird in Kleingruppen diskutiert. Hinweis auf die *Word bank*.

Lösungsvorschlag **a)** *In the first five stanzas the viewpoint is that of a small child who wants to find out what happened to the elephant whose head had been cut off by Shiva in order to save his son Ganesh's life. Whereas the thoughts of the lyrical I as a child circle around the question of how the elephant could possibly have survived, in the second part of the poem (ll. 24 ff.) the adult lyrical I envisions a "rotting carcass of a beheaded elephant" (ll. 27 ff.) and focuses on the consequences of the death of the elephant on his relatives, for instance. Here the viewpoint is* *that of a disillusioned grown-up who no longer indulges in innocent childhood fantasies but whose thoughts are much darker. The lyrical I in the second part of the poem seems to have acknowledged the harsh realities of life and come to terms with them.*

b) *The Hindu concept of the cosmic cycle is reflected both in the structure and the content of the poem. In the first part of the poem a chain of questions illustrates how one life is linked to another (ll. 9–19). The run-on lines in the second part of the poem, on the other hand, highlight the circular movement of life. This image resembles the elephant herd turning and turning in a circle, bemoaning the deceased elephant (ll. 40 ff.). Words like "curiosity", "imagination", "fantasy" and "story" (ll. 4–8) draw to the childhood memories and the "what-if"-mood of the adolescent lyrical I. Images like "rotting carcass of a beheaded elephant lying crumpled up … covered with bird shit, vulture shit –" (ll. 28–31) illustrate the disillusionment of the adult lyrical I who seems to be sorry for the mourning relatives of the elephant. This is stressed by an alliteration in ll. 38–39: "They stared … with their slow swaying sadness …".*

c) *The first part of the poem abounds in questions, reflecting the child's curiosity as to the fate of the beheaded elephant. In contrast to that the second part of the poem only contains statements by which the lyrical I stresses the harsh reality of death.*

d) *A possible interpretation of the last three lines: After the death of a beloved person, the relatives can take no consolation in the notion that the entire life is determined by the cycle of repeated births and deaths.*

Evaluation

3 [👥] *Do your own research on one of the following themes and …*

Die S bereiten in Einzel- oder Partnerarbeit zu Hause Kurzreferate zu den angegebenen Themen vor und präsentieren ihre Ergebnisse im Plenum

Lösungsvorschlag Individuelle S-Beiträge.

Novel excerpt

A visual dialect

pp. 12–13

HINTERGRUNDINFO

*The **caste system** in India is called jati, which refers to the notion of kinship group or lineage. The term itself can be equated with subcaste. It is estimated that there are more than 3,000 jatis in India, each of these having its own customs and traditions, rules and way of life. There is no one all-Indian system of ranking them in a firm hierarchy, but in each local area jati ranking exists and is very much related to purity and pollution. Members of particular castes are allowed to socialise or marry only within their own groups. As the jati system has not been static, mobility has enabled different jatis to move up in the social hierarchy in the course of time.*

*The original Hindu system of caste (derived from the Portugese word "casta", meaning race) was based on ancient religious texts. Indian society was divided in four groups: the highest-ranking caste comprised the **Brahmins**, who were considered as the intellectual and spiritual guides, priests and philosophers. Second were the Kshatriyas who served traditionally as soldiers and administrators. Beneath them were the Vaishyas who were the artisan and commercial class; and the lowest caste were the Shudras who comprised labourers, craftsmen and peasants. It is said that the Brahmin come from Brahma's mouth, **Kshatriyas** from his arms, **Vaisyas** from his thighs, and **Shudras** from his feet. The untouchable or Panchamas were placed below the four main castes. They were not considered as part of human society, but instead as something less than human. They had to do the most menial and degrading jobs and were not to mingle with members of the other castes. The caste system in India is predominantly associated with Hinduism. However, caste lines do exist in Indian Muslim life or among Indian Christians, for example.*

*Since 1949 the Indian Constitution has outlawed the practice of **Untouchability** and has granted all its citizens equal rights and opportunities. However, social change has been gradual. The Indian Government has introduced special quotas in schools and Parliament to support the lowest jatis. There are also laws prohibiting caste discrimination in the field of employment or in the educational sector. However, the caste system itself is not illegal and is maintained in many areas of life in India. Due to economic* *growth, globalisation, improvement in education and similar factors, the caste system particularly in metropolitan India, however, is not as rigid as it was in the past. Upward mobility and the improvement of one's status by professional and financial success are possible now. The majority of the former untouchables, who now call themselves* ***Dalits*** *(the oppressed), are still underprivileged. Approximately 18–20% of the population belong to that group. Many of them suffer from poverty, deprivation, lack of education, food, healthcare, and economic opportunity.*

Lernwortschatz *to scorch, scrub, to grit, shrub, thicket, thorn, to encroach (upon), to billow, muttonchop whiskers, mountainous, to mislead, ridge, to perch, bluff, conical, thatched roof, to lurch, repression, well, to provide, bucket, to admit so. to sth, to enable sb to do sth, smallholder, moustache, knot, coarse, anklet, pinstripe, rigidity, restrictive, divine, serfdom, reassuring, previous, to reward, pious, to defy, to commit oneself to sth*

Materialien → **Online-Link: 601006-0005**

Comprehension

1 *Compare and contrast what Dalrymple sees …*

Die S notieren für Aufgabe **a)** relevante Textstellen in zwei Spalten *(British travel writer/ Dr Tyagi)*. Die Ergebnissicherung erfolgt gemeinsam im Kursgespräch. Teilaufgabe **b)** eignet sich für Partnerarbeit. Hinweis auf die *Fact file* zu Rajasthan.

Lösungsvorschlag

a) *The British travel writer William Dalrymple admires the villages and the inhabitants defying the harsh living conditions and the gradually approaching desert. He notices the women in their colourful saris and the huge turbans and muttonchop whiskers of the tribesmen (ll. 8–10). To him, these details provide a "good, and natural, and harmonious" (ll. 11 ff.) picture.*
Dr Tyagi, on the other hand, points out that the different colours of people's clothes or the way the men trim their moustaches indicate the social rank of an individual. Whereas Dalrymple considers the circular mud huts standing at a distance from a small white-stone village a very pleasant sight (ll. 16 ff.), Dr. Tyagi sees beyond the houses and draws his attention to the fact that the different building material indicates the different social status of the inhabitants. The two different kinds of houses stand separately as the Rajputs, who live in the stone village, and the Harijan, who are confined to the huts, are not allowed to live together. Thus for him the outline of the village is a clear sign of "repression and caste-apartheid" (ll. 21 ff.).

b) *The term 'visual dialect' implies that in India there is communication beyond language. Particular items and especially colours indicate the social rank of a person in the caste system. The meaning of these items and colours changes from region to region but according to Dr Tyagi, "caste was an open book which could be read as soon as you knew the local visual dialect" (ll. 35 ff.). If a man wears a white turban around Jodhpur, he could be identified as a member of the middle castes; if he wears a saffron turban, people would recognise him as a Brahmin. The way men trimmed their moustaches or "the knot with which you tied your dhoti defined you even more closely, and could show even your sub-caste" (ll. 43–44). Women distinguish themselves by the colours and jewellery they wear. Lower-caste women have to wear simple jewellery and darker colours as well as coarse cloth whereas upper caste women used blue, for instance.*
The author makes use of these examples to illustrate the fact that each minor detail is no sheer coincidence but a manifestation of the caste system. The different colours, for example, which a foreign eye might mistake for a sign of the brightness and variety in Indian society, enable natives of the region to place an individual in the correct position in the intricate Indian caste system. By naming many different examples to prove that point, the author makes the reader aware of the all-pervasiveness of the 'visual dialect' in many parts of India.

Analysis

2 *Explain the stabilising effect of the caste system …*

Zunächst individuelle Lektüre der *Fact file* zu *The history of the caste system in India*. Mögliche vorbereitende **Hausaufgabe**; Diskussion in Kleingruppen.

Lösungsvorschlag *According to the text, the Indian caste system also has a stabilising effect on society. Members of each caste and sub-caste definitely know where their place in the social hierarchy is. They are aware of what is appropriate and accepted for a member of their group and what is not. As there are about 3,000 of these social groups, a closely-nit network is established which keeps the country together and serves as "a protection against anarchy" (l. 60). What's more, the caste system might cause the majority of devout Hindus to lead an ethically good life, as "they believe that your caste in this life is determined by your actions in a previous one. A good life is rewarded by high caste, a bad life punished by untouchability" (ll. 63–64).*

View on the stabilising effect of the caste system on society
Individuelle S-Antworten.

Evaluation

3 *Comment on the idea that there is a 'caste system of sorts' in the West.*

Zusatzmaterial → **Klausurvorschlag 1 • Revision file 1**

Lösungsvorschlag ***Aspects students might mention***

- *a more appropriate term for Western societies might be "class system"*
- *social class is predominantly determined by birth, education, occupation, income, etc.*
- *belonging to a certain social class might have implications on where and how you live, who you meet or marry, the way you talk (accent), your influence in the community, your general outlook on life, etc.*
- *many Western societies seem to be class-conscious but no longer class-ridden, i.e. class is an important but not a vital aspect of Western societies*
- *social mobility is possible; thus the class system is open rather than a rigid and firm institution*
- *Western governments are making great efforts in diminishing differences between the social classes (cf. tax policy; education; social welfare programs, etc.)*

Erweiterung Zum Abschluss des *Topics* füllen die S *Revision file* 1 (Themenheft, Seite 60) aus. Ein Lösungsvorschlag befindet sich hier im Lehrerbuch auf Seite 109.

Topic 2: The wounds of history

pp. 14–25

Didaktisches Inhaltsverzeichnis

Bearbeitungszeitraum: 12–14 Unterrichtsstunden

Textsorte / Thema	Unterrichts- methoden	*Input boxes*	Kompetenzen	Textproduktion
Timeline (416 words) / [2◉] [3◉] **Mark Tully's India** (352/362 words)				SB, Seite 14, LB, Seite 22–24
Timeline, interviews/ British rule in India	*Transcripts (352/362 words)* Kursgespräch Online-Link: 601006-0006 Zusatzmaterial: Kopiervorlage 4		Orientierungswissen Leseverstehen Hörverstehen Gespräche führen	*Learning about history Taking notes Comparing aspects*
Why can't we be friends?, 1924 (519 words)				SB, Seite 15, LB, Seite 25/26
Novel excerpt/India during the British Raji	Kursgespräch Gruppenarbeit Zusatzmaterial: Kopiervorlage 5	*VIP file: E. M. Forster*	Leseverstehen Gespräche führen Argumentieren	*Analysing a relationship Examining aspects*
Father to a nation, stranger to his son, 2007 (844 words)				SB, Seite 16/17, LB, Seite 27–29
Newspaper article/ Mahatma Gandhi and his eldest son	Kursgespräch Partnerarbeit Gruppenarbeit Online-Link: 601006-0007 Zusatzmaterial: Kopiervorlage 6	*VIP file: Mohandas Karamchand Gandhi Word bank: Talking about contrasts*	Leseverstehen Gespräche führen Argumentieren	*Evaluating a conflict Taking notes Acting out a dialogue Writing and acting out a film scene*
Cracking India, 1991 (452 words)				SB, Seite 18, LB, Seite 29–31
Novel excerpt/ The Partition of India	Kursgespräch Partnerarbeit Online-Link: 601006-0008	*VIP file: Bapsi Sidhwa Tipp*	Leseverstehen Gespräche führen Argumentieren	*Making a grid Interpreting a question Writing a letter*
Spot on facts: Indian independence (431 words)				SB, Seite 19, LB, Seite 31–33
Factual information/ The two independent states of India and Pakistan	Kursgespräch Partnerarbeit		Leseverstehen Gespräche führen Argumentieren Recherchieren	*Explaining a relationship Giving a comment*
Exit wounds – The legacy of Indian Partition, 2007 (910 words)				SB, Seite 20/21, LB, Seite 33–35
Newspaper commentary/ The legacy of Partition	Kursgespräch Online-Link: 601006-0009	*VIP file: Pankaj Mishra Word bank*	Leseverstehen Gespräche führen Argumentieren	*Summarising main points Discussing views Analysing characters Writing an introductory paragraph*

Textsorte / Thema	Unterrichts-methoden	*Input boxes*	Kompetenzen	Textproduktion
Muslims – India's new 'untouchables', 2008 (933 words)				SB, Seite 22/23, LB, Seite 35/36
Newspaper article/ Muslims in India	Kursgespräch Partnerarbeit	*Word bank: Disagreeing politely in a formal letter*	Leseverstehen Gespräche führen Argumentieren Recherchieren	*Collecting information* *Commenting on the context* *Writing a formal letter*
[2] **Looking across the border, 2006** (499 words)				SB, Seite 24/25, LB, Seite 36–38
Book excerpt/The India-Pakistani border	Kursgespräch		Orientierungswissen Leseverstehen Hör-/Sehverstehen Argumentieren Recherche	*Taking notes* *Comparing aspects* *Considering a perspective*
Indische Presse bezichtigt Pakistans Geheimdienst der Terrorhilfe, 2008 (311 words)				SB, Seite 25, LB, Seite 38
German Internet news article/The relationship between India and Pakistan	Kursgespräch Online-Link: 601006-0010 Zusatzmaterial: Klausurvorschlag 2	*Fact file: The Islamic Republic of Pakistan*	Leseverstehen Argumentieren Gespräche führen Recherchieren Mediation	*Summing up the main points* *Commenting on the contents* *Researching information* *Giving a presentation*

Unterrichtsverlauf

Timeline/Radio broadcasts

Lead-in: The wounds of history p. 14

HINTERGRUNDINFO

History

India was home to several ancient civilisations and empires; one of the earliest of these, the Indus Valley civilisation, flourished on the Indian subcontinent from c. 2600 B.C. to c. 2000 B.C. At around 1500 B.C. the Aryans entered India from the northwest. They introduced Sanskrit and the Vedic religion, a forerunner of Hinduism. Buddhism was founded in the 6th century B.C. and was spread throughout northern India, most notably by one of the great ancient kings of the Mauryan dynasty, Ashoka (c. 269–232 B.C.), who also unified most of the Indian subcontinent for the first time.

*In **1526**, Muslim invaders founded the great Mughal Empire, centred on Delhi, which lasted, at least in name, until 1857. Akbar the Great (1542–1605) strengthened and consolidated this empire. The long reign of his great-grandson, Aurangzeb (1618–1707), represents both the greatest extent of the Mughal Empire and the beginning of its decline.*

*In the **16th century** the Portuguese held a monopoly over the Indian and far-Eastern trade with Europe, after Vasco da Gama had arrived on the coast of modern-day Kerala in 1498, having sailed around the Cape of Good Hope. The Portuguese, however, did not have the resources to maintain a worldwide empire and after the arrival of the British and French they were quickly eclipsed. In **1600** a London trading company was granted a monopoly on British trade with India by Queen Elizabeth I in an English Royal Charter. In **1613** the East India Company, an early English joint-stock company, established its first trading post and for almost 250 years this commercial trading company "ruled" over British India. The East India Company traded mainly in cotton, silk, indigo dye, saltpetre, tea, and opium.*

*By the early **19th century**, India was effectively under British control and the East India Trading Company expanded its territories. Various Indian states remained nominally independent and were governed by their own rulers, the maharajas and nawabs. These "princely states" had an administration of their own while for the remaining country a system of central government was set up.*

*In **1784** the British Parliament established a control board to limit the Company's power although the national administration of the land still lay in the hands of the East India Company until **1858**, when it was dissolved. In that year the administration of India was formally transferred to the British Crown following the Sepoy Mutiny of native troops in 1857–1858. The 1858 Government of India marked the beginning of the British Raj, an expression primarily referring to the British rule in the Indian subcontinent between 1858 and **1947**. The Crown took over the rule with a Secretary of State for India and a Council of India in London. In Calcutta, the Viceroy (i.e. the royal official who governed the country on behalf of and as representative of the monarch) was the head of the central government of British India while the subordinate provinces each had their own governor. At that time India consisted of British India and over 600 native states governed by Indian princes who ruled under the paramountcy of the British Crown. The central government held power over the larger native states whereas the remaining states were under provincial government. In **1876** Queen Victoria became Empress of India.*

*The **19th century** also saw the opening up of India to private investment and missionaries, which was promoted by the British Parliament. Trade and profit remained the main focus of British rule in India, which brought about fundamental changes, both positive and negative. During the Industrial Revolution the vast railway network that is still in use today was set up, in addition to various other developments in the infrastructure. English was imposed as the official language of administration. The British Empire was flourishing at that time: Britain imported raw materials from its colonies and exported manufactured goods to them. India was considered the "Jewel in the Crown of the British Empire". In the late 19th century first steps were taken toward self-government in British India. Indian counsellors who gave advice to the British viceroy were appointed and provincial councils with Indian members were set up. With the Indian Councils Act of 1892 the British subsequently widened participation in legislative councils.*

*In **1885** the Indian National Congress (also known as the Congress Party, INC) was founded. It became the leading force of the Indian Independence Movement. In **1906** the political party All India Muslim League (AIML) was founded at Dhaka by Muslims who resented the Hindu majority in the Indian National Congress. Later the party became the driving force behind the creation of Pakistan as a Muslim state on the Indian subcontinent. In **World War I** India sent more than six million troops to fight* *beside the Allies and provided money for the war. In the after-war years Indian nationalists' unrest gained momentum under the leadership of the Hindu lawyer Mohandas Karamchand Gandhi, generally called Mahatma ("Great Soul") Gandhi. His philosophy of civil disobedience called for non-violent non-cooperation against British authority. He soon became the leading spirit of the Indian National Congress Party, which headed the movement for India's independence. Along with the desire for independence, tensions between Hindus and Muslims had also been increasing over the years. The Muslims had always been a minority, and the prospect of an exclusively Hindu government made them wary of independence; thus they were as inclined to mistrust Hindu rule as they were to resist the Raj. In* ***1919****, the British gave more responsibility to Indian officials, and in* ***1935*** *the Government of India Act granted India a federal form of government and a measure of self-rule. The Muslim minorities received particular protection. In* ***1937*** *nationwide elections were held for the provincial assemblies. Without the consent of Indian leaders the Viceroy declared war in* ***1939*** *and was supported by Muslim leaders against the protest of Congress. In* ***1940*** *the Muslim League officially promoted the idea of a separate Muslim territory (Lahore/Pakistan Resolution) which the Congress strongly rejected. Thus violence between Hindus and Muslims ensued. In* ***1942*** *Mahatma Gandhi started his "Quit India" movement: Gandhi had declared that India could not participate in a war that was ostensibly being fought for democratic freedom, while that freedom was denied to India itself. As the war progressed, Gandhi intensified his demand for independence, drafting a resolution calling for the British to quit India. The draft demanded India's complete independence from Britain and called for civil disobedience if the British did not accede to the demands. One day after the publication of the resolution Gandhi and further major leaders of the movement were imprisoned. Large-scale protests and demonstrations were held all over the country and strikes were called. Violence escalated when bombs exploded, government buildings were set on fire and infrastructure was destroyed. The British arrested more than 100,000 people throughout the country. By early* ***1946*** *Britain adopted a political dialogue with the Indian National Congress for the eventual transfer of power and in August* ***1947****, India gained full independence. However, the predominantly Muslim regions of the north were partitioned into the separate nation of Pakistan. The Muslim League, led by Mohammed Ali Jinnah, demanded a separate nation for the Muslim minority to prevent Hindu political and social domination. Lord Mountbatten as viceroy partitioned India along religious lines and split the provinces of Bengal and the Punjab, which both nations claimed. Thus, when Pakistan was created, it consisted of an eastern and a western part. The Partition of India led to the largest migration in human history, with 12–17 million people fleeing across the borders in both directions to escape the bloody riots that occurred among sectarian groups. Armed conflict also broke out over rival claims to the princely states of Jammu and Kashmir. Jawaharlal Nehru, nationalist leader and head of the Congress Party, was made Prime Minister. In* ***1949****, a constitution was approved, making India a sovereign republic. Within a federal structure the states were organised along linguistic lines. India has fought several wars with Pakistan. The third one resulted in the creation of Bangladesh (formerly East Pakistan) in 1971. Both India and Pakistan possess nuclear weapons. Their relationship remains problematic, as the latest example shows: India accuses the Pakistani intelligence agency ISI of having supported the 2008 terrorist attacks in Mumbai. There have also been boundary disputes with China in the northern part of India, but relations with China are improving gradually.*

Sir Mark Tully*, also known as "The Voice of India", is a radio journalist, author and expert on India who, during his 22-year tenure as the BBC's India Correspondent, reported critically and incisively on the Indian subcontinent. Mark Tully was born in Calcutta in 1935 and raised by a strict European nanny before he was taken to Britain at the age of ten. He was educated at Marlborough public school and Cambridge and then became the BBC India correspondent in 1964. From 1972 to 1993 he was the head of the BBC's Indian Bureau in New Delhi. Tully was made an Officer of the Order of the British Empire in 1985 and was knighted in the 2002 New Year Honours. Tully is also the author of various books on India.*

Lernwortschatz *East India Trading Company, control board, to restrict, expansion, territory, investment, missionary, infrastructure, to import, to export, raw material, manufactured goods, to resent, taxation, interference, inheritance, to impose sth on sb, to abandon, outbreak of violence, act, The British Raj, to dissolve, subordinate, governor, to consist of, empress, counsellor, congress, council, administration, to elect, participation, legislative, assembly, election, to dominate, consent, to support, to object, to ensue, to quit, escalation, withdrawal, to partition*

Materialien → **Online-Link: 601006-0006 • Kopiervorlage 4 (What do you remember about India's past?)**

Der geschichtliche Abriss zur britischen Herrschaft über Indien informiert die S über die wichtigsten historischen Entwicklungen vom 16. Jahrhundert bis zur Teilung von *British India* und zur Unabhängigkeit Indiens. Vorbereitend können einzelne S oder Kleingruppen einen bestimmten Zeitabschnitt mit Hilfe einer PowerPointPräsentation aufbereiten und im Plenum präsentieren, sodass der Kurs einen tieferen Einblick in die historischen Gegebenheiten erhält.

Erweiterung Als Ergänzung kann die *timeline* in **Kopiervorlage 4** (Seite 78) herangezogen werden.

Comprehension

1 [2] *Listen to track two and take notes to answer ...*

Materialien → **CD, Track 2 (Interview: Mark Tully's India – Part 1)**

[2] L präsentiert **Track 2** zweimal von der CD. Das *Transcript* befindet sich als PDF auf der CD.

Lösungsvorschlag

a) ***Information about the events in 1947***

- *Riots started in Punjab on both sides of the new border on the very day that the British Raj was closed in Delhi and Nehru dedicated himself to the service of the Indian people.*
- *Estimates on the number of victims range from 200,000 and 400,000 to even a million.*

How Tully's family experienced these events

- *Tully's father, who had left India just before Partition, and who had always intended to return to England, like many Calcutta businessmen thought that Partition was inevitable but too soon for the Indian people.*
- *Tully's father believed that India was never a real home to the British, who came to India to do business or build bridges, to rule or administer justice, and then retired to some nice seaside resort or remote village in England.*
- *Tully's nursery boy (servant) Jaffa was killed in riots in Bengal.*

b) *"Going jungly" or "going native" means that British citizens living in India adopt an Indian lifestyle, some of them even getting married to a native Indian. Most British people disapproved of that. Tully's grandmother even considered this behaviour as an unforgivable crime.*

Comprehension

2 [3] *Listen to track three and take notes.*

Materialien → **CD, Track 3 (Interview: Mark Tully's India – Part 2)**

[3] Die S hören jetzt **Track 3** von der CD zweimal an. Das *Transcript* des Hörtextes kann ebenfalls herangezogen werden. Es steht auf der CD als PDF zur Verfügung.

Lösungsvorschlag

Notes

- *now 50th anniversary of India's independence*
- *Tully still living in India, so he has broken with family tradition*
- *reports from India for the BBC*
- *speaks Hindi and loves living in India*
- *reporting from India is difficult because of bad communication*
- *although India is a very complicated country, Tully loves the combination of feeling thoroughly at home there and yet knowing that every day you're going to learn more things and knowing that you really know hardly anything at all*

Relation between the first and second part

- *Time: The first part contained Tully's memories of when he made a programme to mark the 40th anniversary of India's independence. The second recording was made ten years later, on the occasion of the 50th anniversary. Place: Tully is still in India.*
- *Communicative situation/content: In the first part Tully reports about the events in 1947 as well as what his father and other Englishmen in India thought about their stay there. In the second part he talks about his personal attitude to life in India. The track also contains an extract from an interview with Tully in which he explains why he has "gone jungly". He even calls it "doing an Uncle Charlie" and thus refers explicitly to what was said in the first track.*

Novel excerpt

Why can't we be friends? p. 15

HINTERGRUNDINFO

Edward Morgan Forster *(1 January 1879 – 7 June 1970), was a renowned English novelist as well as a writer of various short stories, essays and librettos. His novels, among them "A Room With a View", "Howards End", "The Longest Journey" or "Where Angels Fear to Tread", reveal in an ironic way class differences in British society in the early 20th century and its attitudes and hypocritical behaviour towards gender and homosexuality. During the First World War, Forster spent three years in Alexandria doing civilian work and he visited India twice, in 1914 and again in the 1920s. Inspired by his experiences in India, he wrote "A Passage to India" (1924), after he had returned to Britain. The novel, which is set during the British Raj and the Indian independence movement in the 1920s, examines the British-Indian relationship. Rather than developing a political focus, the plot evolves around the friendship between an Indian doctor, Dr Aziz, and a British headmaster, Cyril Fielding, during a trial against the doctor. This trial, and its run-up and aftermath, reveal the prevalent racial tensions and prejudices between Indians and the British at that time.*

Lernwortschatz *Raj, stirrup, to rear, gravestone, to jeer, rein, ancestors, to fit in , drab, to mock, to get rid of sth/ sb, affectionately, to swerve*

Comprehension

1 Describe and analyse the relationship between Aziz and Fielding …

Diese Übung eignet sich nach dem gemeinsamen Lesen im Plenum für eine Partner- oder Kleingruppenarbeit. Einzelne S werden aufgefordert, ihre Ergebnisse auf Folie festzuhalten und sie anschließend dem Kurs zu präsentieren. Hinweis auf die *VIP file* zu E. M. Forster.

Lernwortschatz *Aziz, a Muslim doctor, seems to be very agitated and angry. He tries to make his horse rear in order to threaten Cyril Fielding, the British headmaster and to emphasise his demand: "Clear out, all you Turtons and Burtons. … Down with the English anyhow." (ll. 2–3, ll. 24–25). Fielding, on the other hand, tries to provoke Aziz even further by mockingly questioning his suggestions and by employing irony in order to show that he is not really convinced of what Aziz demands (l. 10, l. 13). Fielding seems to be quite condescending and disparagingly illustrates how unimportant he considers India's role as a nation to be (ll. 20 ff.). His remarks reveal a certain contempt for Aziz's attitude, which makes Aziz even more furious (ll. 23 ff.). His threat "… if it's fifty or five hundred years we shall get rid of you, yes, we shall drive every blasted Englishman into the sea …" (ll. 27–28), however, finally ends in an affectionate prediction "… you and I shall be friends" (l. 29). Aziz's advance ("half kissing him", l. 29) makes Fielding ask "Why can't we be friends now?" (l. 30), a question which he reinforces by embracing Aziz and stressing "It's what I want. It's what you want" (l. 31). This dialogue reveals the ambiguity of both men's feelings towards each other. Although they totally disagree on how India's future should be shaped, they do like each other and show affection for each other. However, the difficult circumstances make it impossible for the two to really come to terms with each other or even become friends, as the last paragraph of this extract suggests (ll. 32 ff.).*

Comprehension

2 Examine important aspects of the text …

Zusatzmaterial **→ Kopiervorlage 5 a–d (Some important literary terms – Part I–IV)**

Diese Aufgabe legt eine arbeitsteilige Gruppenarbeit nahe. Es werden vier Gruppen gebildet, die die unterschiedlichen Aspekte in intensiver Textarbeit analysieren und im Anschluss dem Kurs präsentieren. Ggf. kann jedes Thema von jeweils zwei kleineren Gruppen bearbeitet werden. Nach der Präsentation der Gruppenergebnisse erfolgt eine Gesamtschau im Plenum. Eine geeignete Aufteilung der genannten Aspekte in Gruppenarbeitsthemen ist:

1. *Genre, plot, theme, structure*
2. *Narrator and point of view*
3. *Characters*
4. *Imagery and symbolism*

Erweiterung An dieser Stelle können unterstützend die **Kopiervorlagen 5 a–d** (Seite 79–82) eingesetzt werden, die den S einführende Informationen z. B. zu *narrator, characters, imagery* usw. geben, und mit deren Hilfe die S ihren Arbeitsauftrag leichter bearbeiten können.

Lösungsvorschlag

1. ***Genre, plot, theme, structure***

- *Novel; extract focuses on the exchange between the Muslim physician Dr. Aziz and the British headmaster Cyril Fielding at the time of the British Raj.*
- *The fictitious characters are representative of the two conflicting parties during British rule in India, the Indians and the British; the verbal exchange of the two men might be typical of the conflict between the two sides.*
- *The plot focuses on the argument between Aziz and Fielding, thus depicting the two opposing attitudes regarding British rule in India.*
- *This extract is concerned with the relationship between Indians and the British; the author wants to point out that although there are animosities and strong negative emotions, the individual people still like each other and want to be friends.*
- *The central theme, the ambiguous relationship between the Indians and the British, is highlighted by the structure of the text: whereas more than two thirds of the extract focus on the conflicting notions of the two men, lines 29–31 hint at their real feelings and suggest that they really want to be friends; however, the last part of the extract illustrates that the circumstances do not allow the formation of a stable friendship.*

2. ***Narrator and point of view***

- *The author makes use of a third-person omniscient narrator who tells the story from the outside and knows about the feelings and thoughts of Fielding and Aziz.*
- *This omniscience becomes obvious when the narrator reveals the protagonists' emotions and inner monologues (e.g. ll. 15 ff, ll. 20 ff.).*
- *The narrator even presents the attitudes of animals and inanimate objects: "But the horses didn't want it … the earth … the temples, the tank, the jail, the palace … they didn't want it …" (ll. 32–36).*
- *The narration is characterised by an impressive immediacy due to this narrative technique and creates a very vivid impression of the relationship between Indians and the British at that time.*

3. ***Characters***

- *The two protagonists are characterised as rather hot-headed and excited (ll. 1 ff., ll. 10 ff.).*
- *Aziz is obviously not able to control himself: "… in an awful rage danced this way and that, not knowing what to do …" (ll. 23–24).*
- *Similarly to the Muslim doctor, Fielding is also described as being in a state of great agitation.*
- *Fielding is also characterised by his frequent use of irony and subtle hints revealing his contempt for Aziz's suggestions (ll. 20 ff.).*
- *Despite all the feelings of rage and their respective aggressiveness, however, both Aziz and Fielding are portrayed as affectionate towards each other (ll. 28–29; ll. 30–31).*
- *The characterisation of the protagonists depicts the ambiguity not only of the relationship between the two men but of the relationship of Indians and the British in general, which seem to be characterised by feelings of hatred, contempt, frustration etc. but at the same time by feelings of respect, affection and even friendship.*

4. ***Imagery and symbolism***

- *The author employs a simile in lines 8–9: "the scenery, though it smiled, fell like a gravestone on any human hope"; the scenery, which also serves as a personification, represents the difficult circumstances under which Fielding and Aziz live at the time of the British Raj and which do not enable them, and Indians and the British in general, to live in friendship and harmony; thus people's hope for a better future will not be realised.*
- *the last paragraph of this extract abounds in allusions to the difficulties that the two men and thus Indians and the British in general will not be able to overcome in order to form a stable friendship: "But the horses didn't want it … the earth … the temples, the tank, the jail, the palace … they didn't want it …" (ll. 32–36).*

Newspaper article

Father to a nation, stranger to his son

pp. 16–17

HINTERGRUNDINFO

***Mohandas Karamchand Gandhi (1869–1948)**, known as **'Mahatma' (Great Soul)**, was the leader of the Indian nationalist movement against British rule, and is widely considered to be the father of the Indian nation. He is acclaimed for his doctrine of non-violent protest to reach political and social progress. Mohandas Karamchand Gandhi was born on 2 October 1869 in Porbandar in Gujarat (western India). In his childhood his mother's devoutness and the Jain traditions of the region greatly influenced Mohandas. Religious tolerance, compassion for sentient beings, vegetarianism and fasting for self-purification were among the most important principles that he absorbed at that time.*

In 1883, 13-year-old Mohandas was married to a 14-year-old girl, Kasturbai Makhanji, in an arranged child marriage, as was the custom in the region. In 1887 Gandhi joined Samaldas College in Bhavnagar (Bhaunagar). After university, he went to London to train as a barrister. He returned to India in 1891 and in 1893 accepted a job at an Indian law firm in Durban, South Africa.

In South Africa, Gandhi faced discrimination directed at Indians. Appalled by the treatment of Indian immigrants there, he joined the struggle to fight for basic rights for them. Gandhi stayed in South Africa for 20 years. He was imprisoned several times during that time. In 1906 Gandhi developed his famous philosophy of satyagraha ("devotion to truth"), a new non-violent way of protesting and redressing wrongs. This philosophy was based primarily on principles of Hinduism, but also on elements of Jainism and Christianity and was influenced by writers including Tolstoy and Thoreau. After the South African government had finally conceded to many of Gandhi's demands, he returned to India in 1915 where he announced a new satyagraha which attracted millions of followers. By 1920, Gandhi was an influential figure in Indian politics. His programme of peaceful non-cooperation with the British included boycotts of British goods and institutions, leading to the arrests of thousands. In 1922, Gandhi himself was sentenced to six years' imprisonment. After two years in prison Gandhi was released, whereupon he withdrew from politics and focused on the improvement of Hindu-Muslim relations, which had deteriorated. In 1930, Gandhi announced a new campaign of civil disobedience in protest at a tax on salt, leading thousands on a "March to the Sea" to symbolically make their own salt from seawater. In 1931, Gandhi attended the Round Table Conference in London, as the only representative of the Indian National Congress. However, In 1934 he resigned from the party and was succeeded by Jawaharlal Nehru. In 1945, the British government began negotiations which culminated in the Partition plan of June 1947. Riots and violence evolved in the months before and after independence. Gandhi was opposed to Partition and he did not join the independence celebrations. Instead, he fasted in Calcutta and Delhi in an attempt to cool down people's heated emotions. On 30 January 1948, Gandhi was assassinated in Delhi by a Hindu fanatic.

Lernwortschatz *to confess, regret, to convince, homeland, partition, independent, entire, to rebel against, morality, to make a stand against sb/sth, to challenge, to trade (in), to import, to urge, goods, to convert, to assassinate sb, extremist, independence, to secure sth, innocence, peace, adherence, nonviolence, to defeat, to inspire, to depict, to reveal, release, to coincide, publication, historian, to make sense (of), high expectations, to be based on, belief, society, individual, necessity, hypocritical, to be true to one's principles, to attend, scholarship, to inquire/to enquire, reluctant, deserving, embittered, to trade in sth, to strain, to advocate, renunciation, to encourage, to reply, to refer to, poignant, inconvenient, truth, to shoot a film, director, understated, humane, to supplement, responsibility, dignity, to stem from, need, to be partial to sb, to neglect sb/sth, fragile, to assume, miracle worker, human being, to be in control of sth, portrayal, to ban, research centre, attempt, to tarnish, humanity, to expose, hostage, to emulate, to put sb on a pedestal, frail, to strive (for/to), to achieve, to worship, caste*

Materialien **→ Online-Link: 601006-0007**

Der Einstieg erfolgt über die Präsentation eines Bildes, evtl. auf Folie, das Mahatma Gandhi zeigt. Die S tragen ihr Vorwissen zur Person Ghandis und dessen Bedeutung für die Geschichte Indiens zusammen. Im Anschluss daran lesen sie die *VIP file*. L gibt weitere Informationen zu Gandhi. Ausgehend von der Überschrift *Father to a nation, stranger to his son* stellen die S Vermutungen darüber an, inwiefern das Vater-Sohn-Verhältnis im Falle von Mahatma Gandhi schwierig sein könnte. Es folgt die individuelle Textlektüre.

Analysis **1 *Describe and evaluate the conflict between Gandhi and his eldest son.***

Zusatzmaterial → **Kopiervorlage 6 (Mother Teresa)**

Aufgabe 1 kann als schriftliche **Hausaufgabe** erledigt werden.

Lösungsvorschlag ***Description of the father-son-relationship***

Harilal Gandhi, the Mahatma's eldest son, spent his life disregarding and protesting against the values and principles of his father. The Mahatma believed that "the needs of the nation were more important than the need of any individual" (ll. 51 ff.) and that each individual had to make sacrifices for the larger good of society (l. 30). Thus in the years the family spent in South Africa, Gandhi's children were schooled at home rather than at a private European school, which made his children angry as they could not answer when their peers asked which school they went to (ll. 31 ff.). However, it was quite difficult for Gandhi's children to meet his expectations and to live by his principles (l. 43). In fact, his eldest son turned into quite the opposite of his father's ideal – he became "an alcoholic gambler trading in imported British clothes" (l. 9) which contrasted with Gandhi's strict morality and his firm opposition against everything British (ll. 7–10). Harilal even converted to Islam and took a new name (Abdullah) before he died in 1948, only shortly after his father's assassination by a Hindu extremist.

Evaluation of the father-son-relationship

It is easily understandable that Gandhi's strict moral principles and his firm positions would evoke opposition on the part of his children. Children do need a role model they can look up to, but especially during puberty they question their parents' values and try to find their own position in life. If Harilal's father did not really try to discuss his viewpoint with his eldest son and only insisted on his son's adhering to his moral principles, I can understand that his son rebelled against his father and eventually became the exact opposite of what his father represented. It is difficult for children to understand why the nation is more important to their father than his own family. Besides, it is definitely very difficult to always live in the shadow of one's father. By doing everything his father could not accept, Harilal probably wanted to draw attention to himself and protest against his father's strict attitude.

Erweiterung **Kopiervorlage 6** (Seite 83) thematisiert das Leben und Wirken von Mutter Teresa und beinhaltet eine Übung zu den Zeitformen und zu *conditional clauses*.

Evaluation **2 [👥] [👥👥] *Discuss what sources of information you would use …***

Aufgabe **a)** eignet sich für eine Diskussion in Kleingruppen, während die S **b)** in Partnerarbeit erledigen. Teilaufgabe **c)** kann als schriftliche **Hausaufgabe** gestellt werden. Hinweis auf die Wendungen in der *Word bank* zu *Talking about contrasts*.

Lösungsvorschlag **a) *Aspects that students might consider in their discussion***

- *First the decision should be made as to whether the film is to be a documentary or a feature film.*
- *It's also important to be aware of how the audience should feel about the story, whether they should learn from the plot, laugh, smile, cry or think about it, or just be entertained.*
- *The film must have a good story centred on the figure of historical importance.*
- *The film should be historically accurate.*
- *The figure should be presented from different perspectives, thus casting a light on various aspects of his/her character as well as his/her role in public.*
- *It must be considered whether it's better to tell the story concentrating on one plot or containing various subplots.*
- *It must be decided whether to present the events in chronological order or to use flashbacks, foreshadowing, a frame story or other narrative techniques.*

b) Protester: *I can't accept that you have made a film denigrating Mahatma Gandhi – after all, Mahatma is one of the most important people that has ever lived and he was a man with strict principles and moral ethics that he always strived to live by.*

Khan: *I completely agree with you on the historical importance of Mahatma Gandhi. However, in my film I am trying to show people that Gandhi was a man after all, with all the weaknesses, worries and doubts that each of us faces. I really don't want to disparage his image, I just want to make him appear more human.*

Protester: *I don't think that Mahatma Gandhi was just a normal person like you and me. He was exceptional and he did extraordinary things for India and its people. Thus a film on him must show how unique he was.*

Khan: *I think that 60 years after his assassination it's important to show Mahatma Gandhi in a more realistic way and not to put him on a pedestal, which would mean that people cannot really relate to him as a person any more. In my view it's vital that people realise that he was an ordinary man who believed in his aims and struggled very hard to reach his goals and that it wasn't always easy for him. When they see him like this, people can learn from his example and eventually make their contribution to making the world become a better place. If he was portrayed as a saint, there would be no point in ordinary people emulating him.*

c) Individuelle S-Beiträge.

Novel excerpt

Cracking India

p. 18

HINTERGRUNDINFO

Bapsi Sidhwa *(born in 1938) is an internationally acclaimed author who was raised in Lahore and who now lives in Houston, Texas. Bapsi Sidhwa started writing when she was in her twenties but had difficulties in getting her work published at first. Together with her family, she emigrated to America in the mid-1980s where she became a professor for creative writing.*
She has received numerous awards for her fiction; her novel ***"Cracking India"*** *(1991) was turned into the much acclaimed film "Earth" (1998). In this novel the story is told through the eyes of a clever, inquisitive 8-year-old girl Lenny, who witnesses the increasing unease in Lahore, the riots, fires and brutal massacres.*

Lahore *is the second largest city in Pakistan after Karachi. After Partition it was made capital of the Punjab province in the new state of Pakistan.*

Muhammad Ali Jinnah (1876–1948)

- *Generally regarded as the founder of Pakistan.*
- *He was the leader of The Muslim League, the party that became the driving force behind the creation of Pakistan as a Muslim state on the Indian subcontinent.*
- *Jinnah served as Pakistan's first Governor-General, the resident representative of the monarch appointed by King George VI of the United Kingdom.*
- *His role in the partition of India: Jinnah shaped the Lahore/Pakistan Resolution of 1940, which promoted the creation of separate state for Muslims and launched a campaign to achieve independence for Pakistan.*

Jawaharlal Nehru (1889–1964)

- *Prime Minister of India from 1947 to 1964: he was the first and is the longest-serving prime minister of India to this day.*
- *His role in the partition of India: he was a charismatic and radical leader in the Indian independence movement who demanded complete independence from the British Empire.*
- *Nehru became a leader of the left wing of the Indian National Congress and then, under the mentorship of Mahatma Gandhi, the party's president.*
- *He is sometimes referred to as the "Architect of Modern India" as his politics fundamentally shaped the country and influence India to this day.*
- *Nehru's daughter, Indira Gandhi, and grandson, Rajiv Gandhi, also served as Prime Ministers of India.*

Allama Sir Muhammad Iqbal (1877–1938)

- *A Kashmiri Muslim poet, philosopher and politician whose poetry in Urdu, Arabic and Persian has been highly acclaimed.*
- *His role in the Partition of India: as one of the most famous leaders of the All India Muslim League he successfully directed his fellow Muslims toward the establishment of a separate Muslim state; his vision inspired the creation of Pakistan.*
- *Iqbal encouraged and worked closely with Muhammad Ali Jinnah.*
- *He was knighted in 1922.*

Tara Singh (1885–1967)

- *A well-known Sikh political and religious leader.*
- *In 1930 he became deeply involved with the civil-disobedience movement and was a leader of the Sikhs' Akali Dal party.*

- *His role in the Partition of India: he guided the Sikhs during the Partition of India; later he demanded an autonomous Punjabi-speaking Sikh nation in the Punjab.*

Louis Mountbatten, 1st Earl Mountbatten (1900–1979)
- *British statesman, naval leader, and the last viceroy of India.*
- *His role in the Partition of India: in his hands lay the diplomatic negotiation of independence for India and Pakistan.*
- *After Partition Louis Mountbatten, who is an uncle of Prince Philip, Duke of Edinburgh and husband to Queen Elizabeth II, became the first Governor-General of independent India (1947–1948).*

Lernwortschatz *affluent, habit, to make sth up, disturbing, godmother, to dig, to venture, to shrink, to dwindle, to encompass, token, devotional, fervor (AE), zealot, prayer, to set about doing sth, ostentatious, to squat, tap, diligent, to scrub, to clear one's throat, scarf, mosque, lawn, to pray, to cram sth into sth, slot, to diminish, untouchable, entrenched, to dehumanize (AE), caste, lofty, to look down upon sb, slave, nuclear family, irrelevant*

Materialien → **Online-Link: 601006-0008**

Der Text wird zunächst einmal im Plenum gelesen oder er wird von den S bereits zu Hause erarbeitet. Hinweis auf die *VIP file* zu *Bapsi Sidhwa.*

Comprehension

1 *Make a grid with the names of all the people mentioned …*

Hinweis auf den Tipp (siehe **Erweiterung**). Die S erledigen die Aufgabe in Stillarbeit oder alternativ als schriftliche **Hausaufgabe**.

Lösungsvorschlag

Name	*Who/What the person is*	*How Partition affects this person*
Lenny	*8-year-old first-person narrator, Parsee*	• *very much disturbed by what adults say about Partition and how they react to it* • *realises that Partition revolves around religious differences and is highly aware of emerging religious devotion of people around her* • *she and her family as members of the Parsee become "irrelevant nomenclatures" (l. 32)*
Ayah	*Lenny's Hindu nanny*	• *shows a new devotional fervor and spends a small fortune on sacrificial offerings to the gods in the temple*
Gandhi, Jinnah, Nehru, Iqbal, Tara Singh, Mountbatten	*result of research and presentation (cf. below)*	• *result of research and presentation (cf. below)*
Imam Din and Yousaf	*Muslims, presumably servants or employees of the family*	• *now take Fridays off in order to go to the mosque after demonstratively cleansing themselves* • *they also pray when the muezzin calls, spreading out their mats on the front lawn*
ice-candy-man and masseur	*Muslims, named by Lenny according to their jobs*	• *like the other Muslims mentioned, they are reduced to their role as adherents of their religion*
Hari, Moti and his wife Muccho, his daughter Papoo	*Hindu untouchables, Moti works as a sweeper*	• *become even more untouchable, which means their caste becomes more obvious and more important*

the Sharmas and the Daulatrams	*Brahmin families, presumably neighbours*	• *are "dehumanised by their lofty caste and caste-marks"*
Nehru	*Brahmin*	• *becomes India's Prime Minister*
the Rogers	*English Christians*	• *feel superior to the Anglo-Indian Pens*
Queen Victoria and King George	*English Christian rulers*	• *the British Crown ceases to rule India*
the Pens	*Anglo-Indian Christians*	• *look down upon all non-Christians*
Godmother, Slavesister, Electric-aunt	*members of Lenny's Parsee family*	• *are reduced to being members of a particular religious group*

Erweiterung Zur nächsten Stunde können die S entsprechend dem Vorschlag in dem Tipp im Internet nach der Rolle der genannten Personen bei der Teilung Indiens recherchieren. Lösungsvorschlag für die Kurzpräsentation: siehe **Hintergrundinfo**, S. 29/30.

Analysis

2 How does Lenny feel about Partition …

Aufgabe 2 eignet sich für eine Erarbeitung in Kleingruppen bzw. als Partnerarbeit.

Lösungsvorschlag *At first Lenny is confused and disturbed by Partition. She obviously thinks that India will literally be broken in two and might result in a break under their house or in their neighbourhood. She comes across names of famous people, like Gandhi, Jinnah, Nehru, Iqbal etc., who she apparently does not know anything about. She realises that Partition revolves around religious differences and that all of a sudden people are labeled as Hindu, Muslim, Sikh or Christian whereas before everybody was "just themselves" (ll. 9 ff.). Lenny is very much aware of the changing behaviour of the people around her and the new religious devotion and fervor these people display. She also takes great interest in the religious rituals of the family's employees. The first-person narrator also realises the changing social position that various people experience and is apparently confused by this. The last question, "What is God?" shows that she wonders what label God might get after all. While the people lived together without giving much thought to the differences between their religions, this question was not relevant at all. There was just one God, not a Christian one, a Muslim one etc. Now, just before Partition, Lenny expects everyone to claim God for themselves, which means that even God may be "partitioned" in a way.*

Evaluation

3 [👥] Creative writing: Imagine you were a Hindu and …

Diese Aufgabe wird am besten als schriftliche **Hausaufgabe** ausgearbeitet. Die S lesen ihre Briefe im Plenum vor und die Mitschüler diskutieren konstruktiv über die jeweiligen Inhalte und sprachliche Qualität der verschiedenen Beiträge.

Lösungsvorschlag Individuelle S-Beiträge.

Factual information

Spot on facts: Indian independence p. 19

HINTERGRUNDINFO

see **Hintergrundinfo**, *pp. 22–23*

Lernwortschatz *in the face of, resistance, consequently, unrest, mutiny, moderate, to found, petition, to grant sb sth, to stall, in the wake of sth, domination, to resolve, deadlock, rioting, bloodshed*

Analysis

1 Explain the relationship between the British, the Indian National Congress …

Aufgabe 1 eignet sich für Partnerarbeit oder eine Erarbeitung in Kleingruppen.

Lösungsvorschlag

Relationship between the British, the Indian National Congress and the Muslim League

- *the British rulers in India had had to cope with resistance, unrest and opposition by the locals since they started to establish their influence in India*
- *with the founding of the Indian National Congress in 1885 the struggle for independence became more organised*
- *originally the Indian National Congress opted for peaceful means in order to expand and secure Indians' rights under British rule*
- *however, by the beginning of the 20th century, the actions against the British became more radical and violent (boycotts of British goods, riots)*
- *as the Congress was dominated by the Hindus, the Muslims, who did not feel represented by the Indian National Congress, founded the Muslim League in 1906*
- *the British, who were not willing to agree to Indian independence, took advantage of the fact that India's independence movement was now split into two parties and played them off against each other*

What finally led to the British withdrawal from India

- *the end of the Second World War and its disastrous results (l. 32)*
- *rising nationalism among Indians (ll. 33 ff.)*
- *mutiny by sailors of the Royal Indian Navy (ll. 34–35)*

→ *the British realised that maintaining their rule in India was no longer possible (ll. 36 ff.)*

Comprehension

2 [💻] *Find out about the two parts of Pakistan and what happened to them.*

Die Themenvorschläge in Aufgabe 2 können als Grundlage von Einzel- oder Gruppenpräsentationen dienen.

Lösungsvorschlag

a) *The two parts of Pakistan and what happened to them*

The modern state of Pakistan is a result of the partition of the Indian sub-continent in 1947. Pakistan, which was created to meet the demands of Indian Muslims who sought independent states for the majority Muslim populations of the eastern and western regions of British India, originally consisted of two parts. The eastern part, which is today Bangladesh, borders on India and Burma and is on the Bay of Bengal; the western part, which is present-day Pakistan, reaches from the Arabian Sea to the Himalayas. In between, the wings were separated by 1600 km of the newly-founded independent India.

In 1956, with the adoption of its constitution, Pakistan became an Islamic republic, a title the country still holds today. However, tensions between the two parts of Pakistan arose immediately after the independence of the country. Bengali East Pakistan was more populous and ethnically homogenous as well as being poorer, particularly as it had been cut off from the traditional Bengali capital of Calcutta (now Kolkata). Pakistan's new rulers, few of whom were Bengalis, aimed at a strong central government and just one national language – Urdu. Eastern Pakistanis, however, wanted Bengali to have equal status. Besides, they complained that the central government, the federal bureaucracy and the main military establishments were all located in West Pakistan. Thus opposition among Bengalis against West Pakistan rose and led to a military conflict in 1971. As a result of the Bangladesh Liberation War (26 March – 16 December 1971) the eastern part with its mainly Bengali-speaking population seceded from the western part with the help of India.

After its independence Bangladesh had to cope with severe famines, natural disasters and widespread poverty, as well as political turmoil and military coups. In 1991 democracy was restored. Since then the country has experienced phases of relative calm and economic progress. Several periods of military rule and political instability have characterised Pakistan's history. It has been involved in three wars with India. Among Pakistan's most urgent problems are ethnic, sectarian and civil-military tensions as well as the high levels of poverty and illiteracy. Pakistan, which in 1998 successfully test-exploded a nuclear bomb, is the world's only Muslim-majority nuclear state.

b) *Since 1947 until today there have been 14 Prime Ministers in India, some of whom held office for only a few months or even weeks (e.g. Gulzari Lal Nanda who entered office on 27 May 1964 and left office on 9 June 1964 or Gulzarilal Nanda, who was the interim Prime Minister of India twice for thirteen days each, in 1964 and 1966). Some Prime Ministers, however, remained in office for a considerable period of time, shaping the country in a profound way. Among them were India's first Prime Minister Jawaharlal Nehru, who is to date the longest-serving Prime Minister (15 Aug 1947 – 27 May 1964) and Indira Ghandi who held the office for three consecutive terms from 1966 to 1977 and for a fourth term from 1980 until her assassination in 1984. She was India's first, and to date only, female prime minister. The incumbent is Manmohan Singh, the 14th Prime Minister of India, and the first since Jawaharlal Nehru to return to power after completing a full five-year term. He is also the first Sikh to hold this political office.*

Newspaper commentary

Exit Wounds – The legacy of Indian Partition

pp. 20–21

HINTERGRUNDINFO

Pankaj Mishra *was born in North India in 1969. He is an acclaimed writer, literary critic and lecturer whose essays have been published in various Indian, American and English newspapers and magazines, e.g. "The New York Times", "The New York Review of Books", "The Guardian", "The Financial Times", "The Washington Post", "Time" or "The Independent".*

Mishra's first international breakthrough came in 1999 with the publication of his novel "The Romantics", which has been translated into eleven European languages. In his literary work and essays Pankaj Mishra, who divides his time between London and India, depicts crucial political and social developments on the Indian subcontinent.

Lernwortschatz *legacy, partition, to divide, nation-state, to descend, implication, consequence, hasty, imperial, retreat, irrevocable, enfeebled, disengagement, to exhort (fml), tempting, to figure out, secular, homeland, to intermingle, sectarian, riot, dignified, withdrawal, assumption of power, absence, to denounce, moral authority, ill-informed, agricultural, industrial, to deprive sb of sth, to condemn (sb to sth), rural, backwardness, to spark, tension, preceding, ethnic cleansing, to consult, to anticipate, national identity, bewilderment, panic, rage, to quit, successor, armed, militia, to roam, to rape, to loot, to be capable of sth, to restore, genocidal cast, savagery, to be confined to, dereliction, to disown, sense of mission, disillusion, to collapse, to assail, expedient (fml), to boost, nationalism, to clash, religious persecution*

Materialien → **Online-Link: 601006-0009**

Dieser Text ist inhaltlich recht anspruchsvoll und bedarf der Einbettung in den historischen Kontext. Vor der Lektüre sollte also noch einmal der geschichtliche Hintergrund erläutert werden und zumindest ein Hinweis auf die Rolle von Lord Louis Mountbatten erfolgen.

Comprehension

1 *Summarise why Partition seemed inevitable to the people in power in 1947.*

Im Zuge der Erarbeitung von Aufgabe 1 werden wichtige Aspekte an der Tafel festgehalten.

Lösungsvorschlag *The British were fundamentally weakened by the Second World War and realised too late that they could no longer maintain their rule over India. In fact, in the course of the 1940s they had gradually lost control over the subcontinent so that they wanted to withdraw as soon as possible (ll. 13–16). Thus they ordered the last British viceroy Mountbatten to prepare for a swift withdrawal within 15 months and transfer power to the Indians, which was a difficult task indeed (ll. 17–21). The dominant party, the Congress Party, considering itself a secular organisation, claimed to represent all four hundred million Indians, which, however, was doubted by many Muslim politicians. They considered the Congress Party to be an upper-caste Hindu party and demanded an independent state for the hundred million Muslim inhabitants who had coexisted with non-Muslims "across the subcontinent's villages, towns, and cities" (l. 27). The British finally believed Partition along religious lines to be the solution which would enable them to leave the country in the shortest possible time.*

Analysis

2 *Point out what mistakes Mishra believes the British to have made ...*

Diese Aufgabe sollte schriftlich in Einzelarbeit erledigt werden. Danach werden die Ergebnisse im Plenum diskutiert. Hinweis auf die *VIP file* zu Pankaj Mishra.

Lösungsvorschlag

Aiming to leave the country as quickly as possible the British ignored some stern realities and difficulties. They ordered the last viceroy Mountbatten to prepare for a swift withdrawal and sent an English barrister, Cyril Radcliffe to determine the future border between India and the new country Pakistan. Having only 40 days to fulfil his task, Radcliffe "did not visit the villages, communities, rivers, or forests divided by the lines he drew on paper" (ll. 39–40). As Radcliffe was not fully aware of "the relation between agricultural hinterlands and industrial centres (l. 41), his decision to divide Bengal on religious lines led to serious economic consequences, as the Muslim majority in the eastern region was not granted Calcutta, the major city in Bengal. Consequently East Pakistan, which later became Bangladesh, was deprived of industrial development for decades to follow (ll. 44 ff.).

Radcliffe's decisions regarding the future borders ignited riots and brutal acts of ethnic cleansing, particularly in Punjab, where "Hindus, Muslims, and Sikhs on either side of the new border suddenly found themselves reduced to a religious minority" (ll. 47). The fact that the new borders had been drawn along religious lines resulted in "bewilderment, panic, and murderous rage" (l. 53), a development which was obviously neither expected by Mountbatten nor the Indian leaders who had advised the British and whose aim was to gain power upon the British withdrawal (l. 54). Another problem ensued because the British Army was divided according to the religious denomination of its soldiers; thus Muslim soldiers were sent to Pakistan, Hindu soldiers to India. However, according to the author, many of the troops soon began to fight alongside their "co-religionists in killing-sprees, giving the violence of Partition its genocidal cast" (ll. 59–60).

The author criticises that the British Army did not interfere in order to prevent the slaughter, presumably because British soldiers had received orders not to leave their barracks and only save British lives. Pankaj Mishra considers this behaviour an "act of moral dereliction" (l. 64) which repudiated the "noble sense of mission" of the British Empire (l. 65).

In the final paragraph of the article the author argues that by advantageously promoting political Islam, Churchill had finally ignited "a global jihad engulfing even distant New York and London" (ll. 72 ff.). Mishra thus indirectly holds the British course of action in the Partition to be responsible for the terrorist attacks in 2001 and 2007.

Analysis

3 *Analyse how Mountbatten, Radcliffe and Churchill are presented in the text.*

Lösungsvorschlag

*The author presents **Mountbatten** as a fairly irresponsible representative of the British imperial administration who, only hours before the official Partition of British India, quietly enjoyed a movie with his wife Edwina while large parts of the subcontinent were plunged into turmoil as millions of Hindus, Muslims, and Sikhs realised the impending results of Partition (ll. 1–7). Moreover, in the ensuing riots and slaughter Mountbatten ordered the British troops not to leave their barracks and only save British lives, which the author considers as morally reprehensible (ll. 64 ff).*

***Radcliffe**, the London barrister whose mission it was to draw the exact lines of the future Indian and Pakistan states within only forty days, is presented as rather ignorant towards the difficulties and problems that his far-reaching decisions would have (ll. 37–47).*

***Churchill** is reported to have violently attacked Mountbatten and accused him of "helping Britain's 'enemies', 'Hindustan' against 'Britain's friends', the Muslims" (ll. 70 ff.) some months after Partition. The author blames Churchill for igniting present-day terrorism because he had advantageously promoted political Islam (l. 72).*

Evaluation

4 *Imagine the article were to be included in an anthology …*

Diese Aufgabe erledigen die S am besten als schriftliche **Hausaufgabe**. Verweis auf die *Word bank*, die den S eine wichtige Hilfestellung bei der Formulierung ihrer eigenen Gedanken bietet.

Lösungsvorschlag *In this article the author Pankaj Mishra, an acclaimed writer, literary critic and lecturer who was born in North India in 1969, first examines why Partition seemed inevitable to the people in power in 1947. He then analyses in great detail which mistakes the British made in the process of quitting India and he points out which consequences, both nationally and internationally, these decisions have had.*

Newspaper commentary

Muslims – India's new 'untouchables'

pp. 22–23

Lösungsvorschlag *to target sb/sth, eerie, to recount , ancestry, according to , to shatter, to thrive, suspicion, backlash, to champion sth, to prosper, to pursue, diaspora, to show off sth, hub, vendor, artisan, to deteriorate, to disenfranchise, tale, humiliating, to resort to, to be worse off, to account for, affirmative, plot, to hatch, to gloss over, frank, to stem sth., discontent, catalyst, to tuck sth somewhere, to replicate, treacherous*

Comprehension

1 *Explain the heading of the article. Collect the information …*

Diese Aufgabe erledigen die S nach dem gemeinsamen Lesen im Plenum am besten als Partnerarbeit.

Lösungsvorschlag *The heading, "Muslims – India's new untouchables" refers to the caste system in which traditionally the untouchables were placed below the four main castes. In India, the majority of the former untouchables, who now call themselves Dalits (the oppressed), are still underprivileged. Many of them suffer from poverty, deprivation, lack of education, food, healthcare, and economic opportunity.*
According to the text, a government report in 2006 proved that the socioeconomic condition of Muslims in India is even worse than that of the Dalit caste (ll. 4 ff.). The unemployment rate among Muslim men and women is considerably higher than among the untouchables, for example (ll. 40 ff.). Besides, almost 50% of Muslims over the age of 46 are illiterate. Muslims even feel compelled to live in ghettos, "fearing for their security" (ll. 34–35) due to the fact that they are often labeled as "anti-national, terrorist and agents of Pakistan" (ll. 36–37), which leaves them in a state of hopelessness and suspicion. These findings were confirmed by what the author herself experienced when she travelled through the country and talked to Muslims. According to the author, Muslims "had become largely disenfranchised, poor, jobless and uneducated" (l. 28) and had suffered "humiliating experiences with bureaucratic, housing, job and educational discrimination" (ll. 31 ff.).

Visualising techniques to present the information: *e.g. diagrams (pie charts or bar charts) illustrating the percentages presented in ll. 41–46; table to compare the situation of Muslims in India today to the social status of the Dalit caste.*

Analysis

2 *Pick out references the writer makes to her own personal feelings.*

Diese Aufgabe wird gemeinsam im Plenum erarbeitet.

Lösungsvorschlag *Hearing about the terrorist attacks in Mumbai, the author is reminded of her stay in the Taj Mahal Palace & Tower Hotel two years before where she was reading the newspaper reports on the difficult situation of India's Muslims. At that time she sadly realised that "Muslims are India's new untouchables" (l. 8) and predicted a violent outburst of Muslim anger if India did not cope with the problem. The author relates her feeling of love and pride for her mother country which she wanted to show off to her 4-year-old son (ll. 23–24). However, when she hears about the discriminating experiences of Muslims first hand, she "was deeply saddened" (ll. 26 ff.).*

The author points out that she has been annoyed by the ignorance of politicians abroad who have "glossed over India's problems" (ll. 55 ff.). She is convinced that only by openly talking about the situation of India's Muslims can there "be any hope of stemming Islamic radicalism and realising true secular democracy in the country" (ll. 62 ff.). By relating her own experiences as an expatriate Muslim visiting her home country and by openly talking about her personal feelings and attitudes, the author emphasises her arguments and makes her points more convincing.

Comprehension

3 *If necessary using a dictionary to help you, paraphrase these expressions: …*

Diese Aufgabe erledigen die S am besten als schriftliche **Hausaufgabe**.

Lösungsvorschlag

- *a spotlight of suspicion (l. 15): the assumption of having done sth wrong, illegal or dishonest is focused on sb*
- *diaspora (l. 23): the community of people from one nation living and working in another country*
- *affirmative-action programs (l. 48): measures to promote equality and avoid and combat discrimination of minorities*
- *hot-button issues (l. 53): topics that are controversially discussed and that people feel strongly about*

Research

4 [💻] [👥] *Find out on the Internet why Kashmir is an issue for …*

Die S recherchieren zusammen mit einem Partner oder in Kleingruppen im Internet und bereiten eine kurze Präsentation vor.

Lösungsvorschlag

Since 1947, when the two new states India and Pakistan were founded, Kashmir has been a constant source of tension. Officially Islamabad demands that the incorporation of the majority Muslim province into either India or Pakistan must be determined by Kashmiris. As Pakistan defines itself as an Islamic state, however, the incorporation of Kashmir seems to be a vital national aspiration. At the same time India's official position is that Kashmir is an "integral part" of India and considers the province as vital to its identity as a secular, multiethnic state. Movements for an independent Kashmiri state, such as the Kashmir Freedom Movement and the Jammu Kashmir Liberation Front, also exist and have many supporters. India and Pakistan fought two wars over the region in 1947 and 1965, and a limited conflict in 1999. In 1989 armed violence broke out between militants and India's security forces and army. At least fifty thousand people have died in political violence in Kashmir since 1989.

Discussion

5 *Discuss to what extent you think a country should be left to solve …*

Die Fragestellung wird kontrovers entweder in Kleingruppen oder im gesamten Kurs diskutiert.

Lösungsvorschlag Individuelle S-Beiträge.

Evaluation

6 *Creative writing: Look again at the 2007 article by …*

Diese Aufgabe erledigen die S als schriftliche **Hausaufgabe**. Hinweis auf die *Word bank* zu *Disagreeing politely in a formal letter*, die den S eine wichtige Hilfestellung bei der Formulierung ihres Textes bietet.

Lösungsvorschlag Individuelle S-Beiträge.

Book excerpt

Looking across the border pp. 24–25

Lernwortschatz *dagger, to perceive, to claim, to relinquish, to propound, sacrifice, pursuit, to abandon, stance, to rectify, to contribute, profound, to subscribe to sth, eventually, merge, remain, intractable, to exacerbate, to stoke, to ensconce, enmity, to be struck by sth, in reverse, allure*

Materialien → Online-Link: 601006-0010

Comprehension

1 While reading: Note down the main ideas in each paragraph …

Der Text wird in Stillarbeit gelesen und die S notieren sich während des Lesens die wichtigsten Inhalte jedes Absatzes in ihr Heft.

Lösungsvorschlag

1st paragraph (ll. 1–9): *The very existence of Pakistan is perceived as a threat by many Indians, firstly because Pakistan claims Kashmir, India's only Muslim-majority province, and presumably will not give up that claim.*

2nd paragraph (ll. 10–19): *Secondly, the partition of India and the creation of two states, India and Pakistan, was and is still considered an unnecessary tragedy by many Indians who think that partition neglected India's natural geographical and cultural boundaries and thus should be rectified eventually.*

3rd paragraph (ll. 20–33): *Thirdly, Pakistan is considered an "existential threat to India's secular identity with the potential of averting the loyalty of India's Muslim minority, who, however, seem to be firmly integrated in India.*

4th paragraph (ll. 34–42): *It seems to be predominantly the Pakistani government and military that make an issue of Pakistan's extreme fear towards its Indian neighbours; direct interaction between ordinary Indians and Pakistanis is usually characterised by mutually friendly feelings towards each other.*

Comprehension

2 [2🎬] The India-Pakistan border is closed every evening.

Materialien → Film 2 (The Border)

[2🎬] Im Plenum stellen die S zunächst ihre Vorstellungen vor. Der Videoclip wird zweimal gezeigt. Beim zweiten Durchlauf machen sich die S bereits Notizen. Auf der Grundlage dieser Notizen bearbeiten sie in Partnerarbeit Aufgabe 2.

Lösungsvorschlag

Students' expectations
Individual answers.

Description of the closing of the border
The border gates are closed to traffic at dusk. By night the border, which by day is an internationally recognised frontier of two rival states, becomes the setting for a show of epic proportions. On both sides of the gates, crowds of people gather in order to watch the gate closing ceremony. Bleachers have been built to accommodate the spectators. Many people dance and sing, others sit on their seats attentively. There is a lot of cheering and music in the air and the scene resembles the atmosphere at a wedding or festival. The national guards are among the crowd, but people do not seem to realise that there are real soldiers with real guns and real bullets on both sides of the border. As the closing of the border ceremony begins, the atmosphere gets at once more solemn and oppressive. One of the guards, who all have impressive moustaches, blows his horn and shouts a signal loudly. Two of the Indian officers in their brownish uniforms, wearing yellow and red helmets with red and golden fans on top of them, march at a brisk pace towards the border. Spectators form an aisle through which the two soldiers march, their legs raised high up into the air, their arms swinging next to their bodies. The crowd cheer as if they were supporting their football team in a stadium. A similar ceremony takes place on the Pakistani side of the border. The Pakistani soldiers, who sport full beards, wear uniforms, too. They also march without turning a hair and swing their legs into the air. Their gait seems similarly aggressive and resolute. The march resembles martial arts, ballet and a military parade. At the border, a Pakistani and an Indian soldier meet, face each other, take a rope and they pull down their respective flags on a signal. The spectators applaud and cheer. The culmination of the ceremony is reached when a Pakistani soldier and an Indian soldier walk towards each other, turn, face each other and briefly shake hands. Then the gates on both sides are closed and the official ceremony has come to an end.

Comparison with students' expectations
Individual answers.

Analysis

3 *Refer to the text and the film to compare and contrast the view …*

Diese Aufgabe eignet sich für eine Erarbeitung in Partner- oder Gruppenarbeit.

Lösungsvorschlag *Obviously there is a difference between the perception of the India-Pakistan border and the division of both countries as far as private individuals and the respective governments are concerned. Edward Luce claims that the paranoia towards the neighbouring country comes mainly from the "military and diplomatic elites in Islamabad" (ll. 37 ff). However, many Indians, in his opinion, consider "the very existence of Pakistan … as a dagger aimed at the heart of India" (l. 12) and enumerates several reasons for this widespread attitude: First of all, Pakistan's persistent claim of Kashmir is considered a threat (ll. 2 ff). Secondly, many Indians obviously feel that India and Pakistan should be reunited at some unspecified point in the future (ll. 13 ff.) as the creation of Pakistan is considered a violation of India's natural geographical and cultural boundaries. Thirdly, Indians fear that Pakistan will endanger the loyalty of India's Muslim minority and thus endanger India's secularism. The author also says that on the basis of individual encounters the relationship between Pakistanis and Indians is characterised by "goodwill and warmth", a claim which is illustrated by the video on the border closing ceremony, too. On both sides of the gates, people seem to be happy and cheerful. They do not seem to be hostile towards each other.*

German Internet news article

Indiens Presse bezichtigt Pakistans Geheimdienst der Terrorhilfe p. 25

Comprehension

4 *The text below is a report on one aspect of the consequences …*

Diese Aufgabe eignet sich als schriftliche **Hausaufgabe**.

Lösungsvorschlag *After the terrorist attacks in Mumbai tensions between India and Pakistan have reached a new dimension. According to some newspaper reports there is some evidence for the involvement of the Pakistani secret service ISI in the attacks in Mumbai. Allegedly Indian national security agencies claim that ISI played an active role in the training of the terrorists. However, the details of the reproaches remain murky. None of the newspapers name the sources of the information but quote anonymous government employees instead. Those sources also claim that the Pakistani military, which is in charge of the security service, had been informed of the terrorist plans whereas the civilian government was allegedly unsuspecting. Observers reportedly consider this as another indication of the serious tensions between the powerful military and the elected government.*

Evaluation

5 *Comment on the contents of the Spiegel article …*

Zusatzmaterial → **Klausurvorschlag 2 • Revision file 2**

Die Fragestellung wird im Plenum besprochen. Hinweis auf die *Fact file* zu *The Islamic Republic of Pakistan*. Mögliche Konfliktfelder, die die S als Thema für eine Kurzpräsentation (Teilaufgabe **b)** wählen könnten: *China – Tibet; North Korea – South Korea; Russia – Ukraine.*

Lösungsvorschlag Individuelle S-Äußerungen.

Erweiterung Zum Abschluss des Topics füllen die S *Revision file* 2 (Themenheft, Seite 61) aus. Ein Lösungsvorschlag befindet sich hier im Lehrerbuch (Seite 110).

Topic 3: Different worlds

pp. 26–35

Didaktisches Inhaltsverzeichnis

Bearbeitungszeitraum: 8–10 Unterrichtsstunden

Textsorte / Thema	Unterrichts-methoden	*Input boxes*	Kompetenzen	Textproduktion
Quotations by Gandhi and Ambedkar (138 words)/[4 ◉] **Mark Tully's India**				SB, Seite 26/27, LB, Seite 40–42
Combination of visuals, quotes, statistics, interview/Rural India vs. city life	*Transcript* (496 *words*) Kursgespräch	*Word bank: Talking about lifestyles* *Tip: Charles Dickens*	Orientierungswissen Bildbeschreibung/ -analyse Leseverstehen Hörverstehen Gespräche führen	*Describing and comparing pictures* *Analysing quotations* *Discussing views*
[3 🎬] **'Long live Suttee', cried the mob, 2002** (770 words)				SB, Seite 28/29, LB, Seite 42–46
Newspaper article, video clip/Widows in Hinduism, the Barefoot College	Kursgespräch Online-Link: 601006-0011 Zusatzmaterial: Kopiervorlage 7	*Fact file: Suttee*	Leseverstehen Hör-/Sehverstehen Gespräche führen Argumentieren Recherchieren	*Summarising facts* *Analysing details* *Explaining phrases* *Taking notes* *Collecting information*
Hunger, 1954 (1168 words)				SB, Seite 30/31, LB, Seite 46–49
Novel excerpt/Life of poor peasants in India	Kursgespräch Online-Link: 601006-0012	*Fact file: The monsoon* *VIP file: Kamala Markandaya* *Word bank: Commenting on style*	Leseverstehen Argumentieren Gespräche führen	*Creating a diagram or flow chart* *Analysing style and tone* *Making a literary translation* *Comparing versions*
The Solitude of Emperors, 2007 (1229 words)				SB, Seite 32/33, LB, Seite 49/50
Novel excerpt/ Living between the castes	Kursgespräch	*VIP file: David Davidar* *Tip*	Leseverstehen Gespräche führen Argumentieren	*Summing up a story* *Comparing aspects*
[4 🎬] **A shocking transformation, 2007** (1044 words)				SB, Seite 34/35, LB, Seite 50–52
Interview transcript, video clip/Changes in India	Kursgespräch Online-Link: 601006-0013 Zusatzmaterial: Klausurvorschlag 3	*Word bank*	Leseverstehen Gespräche führen Hör-/Sehverstehen	*Analysing and summing up facts* *Comparing aspects*

Unterrichtsverlauf

Photographs/ Quotes/Statistics

Lead-in: Different worlds pp. 26–27

HINTERGRUNDINFO

Bhimrao Ramji Ambedkar *(14 April 1891 – 6 December 1956) was born into an untouchable family but overcame all odds and received a college education in India. He attained law degrees and doctorates in economics and political science from Columbia University and the London School of Economics. Ambedkar dedicated his life to the struggle against social discrimination and the Hindu caste system. He was also one of the main architects of India's constitution of 1950 which abolished the caste system and guaranteed legal equality to all individuals regardless of caste.*

*For **Mahatma Gandhi** see* **Hintergrundinfo**, *p. 27.*

Jawaharlal Nehru *(14 November 1889 – 27 May 1964) was the first prime minister of India. His father, a barrister and Indian politician, sent him to Great Britain to be educated, first to Harrow School followed by Trinity College at the University of Cambridge. He was a leading figure of the Indian independence movement under the mentorship of Mahatma Gandhi. The leader of the left wing of the Indian National Congress he was a charismatic and radical advocate of complete independence from the British Empire. He was elected by the Congress Party to become India's first and longest serving prime minister from 1947 until 1964. In the latter years his government was criticised harshly because of the lack of defence against Chinese invaders. He died in 1964 of a heart attack.*

Charles Dickens *(7 February 1812 – 9 June 1870) was an English author of the Victorian era who wrote numerous highly acclaimed novels including David Copperfield, Oliver Twist or Great Expectations. The author's work focused on the theme of social reform. He depicted the social classes, mores and values of Victorian England and brought awareness to the plight of the poor and the injustices in the English society of that time.*

Lernwortschatz *convinced, to attain, to recognise, recourse (fml), to resort to, infinite, ignorance, narrow mindedness, communalism, bustee (Hindi)*

Comprehension

1 *Outline what the photos tell you about rural and urban life in India.*

Aufgabe **a)** wird nach einer kurzen Stillarbeitsphase, in der sich die S Notizen zu den jeweiligen Fotos machen, im Plenum besprochen; Teilaufgabe **b)** eignet sich für Partnerarbeit.

Lösungsvorschlag

a) *As the title of topic 3 suggests, rural and urban life in India seem to be worlds apart. The stark contrasts between life in the country and life in the city are illustrated by the photographs. All the photos that depict city scenes suggest that India's urban life is bustling, full of life and modern. The photo at the top left hand corner shows a street presumably during the rush hour: various cars and motorcycles are in a traffic jam; the pavement is crowded; billboards can be seen all over the place. In the middle of the collage the photo of a modern cinema with an advertisement for a Bollywood film indicates the important role of the entertainment industry in India. In two photographs high-rise buildings can be seen in the background. However, in the photograph in the lower left hand corner, a woman in a sari is heating up something in a cauldron, sitting on a heap of garbage against the background of the silhouette of a modern city. In another picture, a bare-footed woman is sitting behind some bowls on the barren ground, a canister next to her. These two scenes are in great contrast to the picture in between, in which an Indian family sharing a meal can be seen. They are sitting at a wooden table, drinking red wine and obviously enjoying various dishes. Rural life is depicted as very hard and physically strenuous in the photographs. In one picture a man is leading a plough or some similar device with two oxen through knee-deep water. In another photograph women are getting water at a well. On the very right a photograph shows a young child and a woman harvesting chilli, obviously also a very exhausting task.*

b) ***pp. 26–27 top, from left to right***
photo 1: Bustling city life

photo 2: Hardships of rural life
photo 3: Bollywood fascination
photo 4: Water – essential and valuable
photo 5: Harvesting chilli

pp. 26–27 bottom, from left to right
photo 1: Living below the poverty line
photo 2: Enjoying a family dinner
photo 3: Being content despite all odds
photo 4: Abundant jewellery
photo 5: High-rise buildings

Analysis

2 Use the visual information together with the statistics above ...

Diese Aufgabe eignet sich für eine Besprechung in Kleingruppen. Hinweis auf die *Word bank* zu *Talking about lifestyles.*

Lösungsvorschlag *India's economic productivity relies heavily on the people who live in the cities; however, their number is less than 28% of the total population. On the other hand, the 65% of the population who depend on agriculture for a living contribute only 25% to the whole economy. Thus, there is a huge difference in economic productivity between the rural and city population of India, which presumably leads to conflicts and difficulties. Moreover, economic productivity might also be slowed down by the problem of illiteracy: the national male literacy rate is 75,9% while the rate for females is only 54,2%.*

The photographs show that the standard of living of the rural population differs extremely from that of the city population. As some pictures suggest, life in the country seems to be very hard. Many people struggle to eke out a living. They hardly have access to public amenities and services. Children, rather than going to school, obviously have to help their families with the crops. They try to make a living from whatever nature provides for them. On the other hand, many people in the cities seem to be quite well-off; they enjoy good quality housing, secure employment and the comfort of a middle-class consumer lifestyle. Some even flaunt their wealth, for example through expensive wedding ceremonies and jewellery. However, there are also a great number of people in the cities who live below the poverty line. According to the statistics, 50% of people in Mumbai live in shanty towns, in open spaces in the city or on the pavements. Moreover, an estimated 150,000 street children live in Delhi, for instance. Mass migration from the country to the cities might be one factor which worsens these problems: between 1991 and 2001 over 70 million people migrated from rural areas to urban areas. Obviously there is not enough affordable housing and regular jobs for these migrants.

Another problem India has to deal with is the conflicting demands on the water supply. Whereas, according to the statistics, India has 17% of the world's population, it only has 4% of its fresh water. Estimations are that domestic water use in urban areas will double by 2025, and industrial use will triple. Thus there will be serious water shortages in the country, worsening the living standard of the rural population.

Comprehension

3 Read the two quotations above and compare the attitudes ...

Die beiden Teilaufgaben **a)** und **b)** eignen sich als schriftliche **Hausaufgabe**.

Lösungsvorschlag **a)** *Mahatma Gandhi believes that the only way of establishing true freedom and peace among people is if people resort to living in villages rather than in towns. He is convinced that living in huts instead of palaces prevents violence and lies, which people would turn to if they lived in cities as tens of millions of people would not be able to live together peacefully in cities. Bhimrao Ambedkar, on the other hand, defines the image of rural Indian life as being something not worth striving for. He considers the love of the intellectual Indian for the village community as pathetic. He equates village life with negative attributes such as "a sink of localism, a den of ignorance, narrow-mindedness and communalism".*

Gandhi's words become more comprehensible if you relate them to his own life as a simple man in peasant clothes who believed that the individual had to back down for the good of the nation. Thus enjoying the amenities and luxuries of city life would be in stark contrast to his credo of a devout, harmonious and simple life, in which the needs of the nation are more important than the need of any individual. This is why he considers the slow pace of life in the villages as a prerequisite for the attainment of peace and freedom in the Indian nation.
The information given about Ambedkar helps to explain his views. He was a Dalit leader, i.e. he represented those people who were traditionally regarded as low caste or untouchables. He was also the main author of India's 1950 constitution which abolished the caste system and gave legal equality to all individuals regardless of caste. His quote illustrates that he thinks life in the village provides for the particular interests of only some people and promotes ignorance and narrow-mindedness among the inhabitants.

b) *Promoting an ideal of simple village life as Gandhi did might deprive people of the amenities and commodities of modern city life. Social mobility might be halted, the chances of education might be diminished. There is little chance of economic and intellectual development. Thus Gandhi's credo that people will have to live in villages in order for India to attain true freedom and peace might have had a negative effect on the development of India.*

Comprehension

4 [4◉] *Listen to Mark Tully talking about the lifestyle of a poor man …*

Materialien → **CD, Track 4 (Mark Tully's India – Part III)**

[4◉] L präsentiert die Tonaufnahme zweimal von der CD. Das *Transcript* des Hörtextes steht auf der CD als PDF zur Verfügung. Hinweis auf den Tipp; ggf. Informationen zu Charles Dickens.

Lösungsvorschlag

a) ***The man's job:*** *Djamla Das shines shoes on the pavement outside the Great Eastern Hotel.*

Where he lives: *Djamla Das lives in a very dark quarter of an old house right in the centre of the city, near the old university college and roughly two miles from the commercial centre of the city. His quarter, which is at the end of a very narrow alley, is a very small place of about eight foot by ten.*

What the conditions are like: *The man's home does not have any apparent ventilation at all. Seven people live in this very, very small room, some people sleep on the floor, and some people sleep on bunks slung from one wall to the other. In one corner of the room the people make their food, in another corner they sleep.*

b) ***The man's attitude towards his fate in life:*** *He accepts his living conditions as his fate which he cannot control or change.*

Why Tully thinks it would be dangerous to talk to him about it: *Tully thinks that until one can actually improve the situation of these people it would be very dangerous to talk about fatalism. Tully believes that the fatalistic attitude is what keeps people alive and able to cope with the situation which would certainly defeat him, and defeat most people.*

Newspaper article/Video clip

'Long live Suttee' cried the mob

pp. 28–29

HINTERGRUNDINFO

*The **status of widows** in some parts of India is a very miserable one. Traditionally Hinduism disapproves of widows remarrying. Many have their social and economic power eroded, too, as they are often excluded and marginalised in the rural villages. Many Hindus link a woman's identity so closely to the man that once he dies, the existence of the widow cannot be accepted any longer. In recent years there have been moves to enhance widows' status, however.*

***Suttee** (also **Sati**) is the practice of a widow immolating herself on her husband's funeral pyre. This rare practice, which today mostly happens in parts of northern and central India, is believed to have originated 700 years ago among the ruling class or Rajputs in India. In order to avoid being* *taken by the victors, the Rajput women burnt themselves after their husbands were defeated in battles. In 1829 the custom was outlawed by India's British rulers following demands by Indian reformers. Cases of suttee are now very rare. The last high-profile incident before Kuttu Bai's suttee in 2002 took place in Rajasthan in 1987 when 18-year-old Roop Kanwar was burned to death. This sparked national and international outrage as well as widespread media attention which led India to enact legislation calling for the death penalty for anyone abetting suttee. It is also illegal to be a bystander at an event of suttee, to glorify or attempt to commit suttee.*

Lernwortschatz *apparently, intention, impending, to gather, to cradle, to drag (off), to blaze, to pelt sb/sth with sth, to keel over, entire, to gain, nondescript, bleak, to allocate, struggle, to insist on sth/to insist that …, estranged, to empower, lot, enviable, to ostracise sb, affluent, to deluge, futile, inevitable*

Materialien → **Film 3 (A visit to the Barefoot College) • Online-Link: 601006-0011**

Comprehension

1 [3] [] *Watch the video once without taking notes. Sum up who …*

[3] Der Videoclip wird zunächst einmal ohne Vorinformationen angeschaut. Danach wird Teilaufgabe **a)** im Plenum besprochen und das Video erneut vorgespielt. Für die Beantwortung von Aufgabe **b)** fertigen die S Notizen im Heft an. Teilaufgabe **c)** eignet sich als schriftliche **Hausaufgabe**.

Lösungsvorschlag

a) *The Barefoot College is for children, who attend night school run by the college, as well as for adults, who are learning practical skills like repairing solar powered lights. Students are from the poor agricultural areas of India but also from countries far away like Ethiopia or Bolivia. Rather than teaching facts and figures, the college aims at teaching equality in this notoriously hierarchical society. At Barefoot one's age, religion or gender don't seem to matter.*

b) 1. *In India's poorest areas, children are more likely to work in the fields than study at school. The Barefoot College, however, wants to change that situation. Thus night school, which is run by the college, enables those children who tend their fields and flocks by day to attain some basic level of education. The Children's Parliament meets once a month. It gives them a chance to give feedback on how their education is going and even on how the schools are run.*
2. *Women are learning how to maintain solar-powered lights, which are very handy in villages with little electricity.*
3. *Everyone seems to learn together very well and everybody eats together, regardless of their language, gender, caste, age or religion. Social equality is the big lesson in the usually very hierarchical society of rural India. Thus the college is steadily encouraging a sense of equality in one of India's most conservative regions.*

c) *The Barefoot College was founded in 1972. It is a non-government organisation whose aim is to provide basic services and solutions to problems in rural India. Among the areas the organisation covers are energy and water supply, education, health care and sanitation, employment of the villagers, social awareness and the empowerment of women as well as the conservation of ecological systems in rural India. The overall aim of the Barefoot College is to turn the rural villages into self-sufficient and sustainable communities.*

Brainteaser

2 *Before reading: India's constitution gives women the same legal rights …*

Zunächst stellen die S im Plenum ihre Vermutungen bezüglich der Aufgabenstellung an, bevor der Text gemeinsam gelesen wird. Hinweis auf die *Fact file* zu *Suttee*.

Lösungsvorschlag

Before or immediately after birth
- *Boys might be considered more valuable and thus female foetuses might be aborted or female babies might be killed shortly after their birth.*

During their childhood and adolescence
- *Girls might not be given the same education.*
- *They might be forced to do menial work whereas boys might enjoy a proper school education.*

- *They might be treated condescendingly and not be taken as seriously as boys by their parents, teachers and other adults.*
- *They might be forced into arranged marriages.*

As adults
- *Women might not be given the same career chances.*
- *They might be forced to do jobs without adequate payment.*
- *They might be discriminated against openly or indirectly by officials, family members etc.*
- *They might be victims of sexual harassment or domestic violence.*

Discussion

3 *Skim the text for the gist and give your immediate reaction.*

Die S verbalisieren im Anschluss an die Textlektüre ihre spontanen Reaktionen im Plenum.

Lösungsvorschlag Individuelle S-Antworten.

Comprehension

4 *Now look at the article again more closely. What information does ...?*

Aufgabe 4 kann in Stillarbeit oder alternativ auch in einer Partnerarbeitsphase bearbeitet werden.

Lösungsvorschlag *According to the text, suttee is a very old Indian custom in which a widow burns herself on her husband's funeral pyre. In the Hindu religion it is believed that a woman can attain god-like status if she dies with her husband (ll. 21 ff.). On the other hand, suttee is obviously "a very shameful act" (l. 46). The text gives several possible reasons why Kuttu Bai committed suttee. One reason might be the hopeless and desperate situation she might have been in after her husband's death (ll. 25 ff.). By contrast, the police surmised that her sons might have killed her because she owned six acres of land (ll. 41–42), a view which is doubted by a delegation of India's National Committee of Women who argue that Kuttu Bai committed suttee voluntarily. A sociologist of Nehru University in New Delhi explains that women face a miserable status as widows as they are not allowed to marry again and are social outcasts who cannot take part in rituals anymore. Thinking that "her life would be one of isolation and despair and shame and suffering" (ll. 52–53), Kuttu Bai seemed to have seen the only solution in committing suttee.*

Analysis

5 [👥] *First talk about any discrepancies or contradictions you notice ...*

Teilaufgabe **a)** wird in Partnerarbeit erledigt, Aufgabe **b)** eignet sich für eine Stillarbeitsphase oder als schriftliche **Hausaufgabe**, Teilaufgabe **c)** wird im Plenum besprochen.

Lösungsvorschlag **a)** *There are obvious contradictions as far as the reasons for why Kuttu Bai committed suttee are concerned. There are also different statements on how the police reacted when they came to the pyre. There are no definite indications on how the pyre was lit. The role of Kuttu Bai's sons is also not really clear. Then there are contradictory statements on the relationship between Kuttu Bai and her husband Mallu Nai.*

List of definite facts
- *Kuttu Bai's husband, a poor barber in rural India, died at the age of 60 from an illness of some kind.*
- *The next morning, his widow, 65-year-old Kuttu Bai, walked up the hill and, in her wedding dress, sat down on her husband's funeral pyre.*
- *A crowd of about 2,000 village people gathered to watch the scene, lit incense sticks and gave Kuttu Bai some betel leaves while she was cradling her husband's head in her lap.*
- *The crowd shouted: "Long live Suttee, our mother" as Kuttu keeled over (ll. 18 ff.).*

List of areas that are open to speculation
- *Did Kuttu Bai willingly announce her intention to commit suttee (l. 6; ll. 44–45) or did her sons murder her (l. 42)?*
- *Did her family want to prevent her from committing suttee (l. 45)?*

- *How did the two local police constables react when they arrived at the scene (ll. 14 ff.)?*
- *How was her husband's pyre lit? Was it her elder son, Ashok, who "finally set light to it (l. 14) or did it catch "fire spontaneously, or with divine help" (ll. 59–60) as the majority in the village say?*

b) *Words, phrases and devices which convey that the writer is not clear about what happened*
- *apparently (l. 5)*
- *there is strong evidence (l. 13)*
- *senior officers claim (l. 15)*
- *other sources say (l. 17)*
- *Why then would she kill herself? (l. 40)*
- *the police speculated (l. 41)*

c) ***Kutta Bai's suttee***

Facts	*Speculations*
• *Kuttu Bai was burnt to death on her husband's pyre after walking up the hill in her wedding dress* • *about 2,000 villagers watched the scene, shouting "Long live Suttee, our mother" after having lit incense sticks and offering the widow some food*	• *reasons for Kuttu Bai's suttee (Voluntary or forced (sons); because of the miserable perspectives for her as a widow?)* • *role of her family (Did they want to prevent the suttee? Did her elder son light the fire? Did her sons murder her?)* • *reaction of the two police officers (Did one of them try to hold her back or simply run away?)*

Analysis

6 Explain what is meant or implied by: a good age by Indian standards …

Aufgabe 6 bietet sich als schriftliche **Hausaufgabe** an.

Lösungsvorschlag
- *a good age by Indian standards (l. 3): quite old, considering the low life expectancy in India*
- *the stuff of controversy and myth (l. 20): a topic which will be hotly debated and embellished and finally become a well-known legend*
- *its statistics are bleak (l. 29): its figures are not encouraging and do not give any reason for hope*
- *money allocated for development has disappeared (l. 31): money that had officially been given to local authorities to improve the situation has vanished*
- *the perversely "empowering" option of suttee (l. 47): deliberately burning oneself to death on the pyre of one's husband, which might seem strange and unacceptable to some, gives the widow a lost chance for control and strength*

Discussion

7 Discussion: Are westerners able to judge traditions or social systems …?

Zusatzmaterial → **Kopiervorlage 7 (An imaginary interview)**

Aufgabe 7 bietet die Grundlage für eine kontroverse Diskussion im Plenum oder in Kleingruppen.

Lösungsvorschlag ***Yes***

There are certain basic human rights as well as actions and modes of behaviour that are universally right and others that are universally wrong, and thus westerners are able to judge or even criticise certain practices or customs of another culture, e.g. if people are tortured, not treated equally or are denied a fair trial. However, it's important to get as much information as possible beforehand as well as undergo continual self analysis and a process of introspection which will help us westerners to understand other societies and cultures on their own terms rather than from a biased viewpoint. Only then will we be able to judge traditions and social systems in another country and culture in a fair way.

No
Westerners cannot apply their standards to the adherents of other cultural and religious systems. Due to different traditions and customs, members of other countries and societies may not agree with us about right and wrong ways of behaviour or about the preconditions we assume to be essential to a worthwhile life. Westerners often only have stereotypical perspectives on other cultures; they look at the world through cultural lenses. The ignorance and the lack of information that we often have in the Western world might only lead to bitter arguments and conflicts if we judge other cultures.

Erweiterung **Kopiervorlage 7** (Seite 84) bietet die Möglichkeit zu einem Rollenspiel in Partnerarbeit. S1 übernimmt die Rolle eines Reporters, der über den *suttee* der Witwe Kuttu Bai schreibt, S2 spielt entweder einen von Kuttus Söhnen, einen Dorfbewohner oder einen Polizisten.

Novel excerpt

Hunger pp. 30–31

HINTERGRUNDINFO

Kamala Markandaya *(1924–2004) is an Indo-British novelist who was born in a small town in Mysore in 1924 to a Brahman family and who settled in England at the age of 25, following her marriage to Bertrand Taylor. Markandaya studied history at the University of Madras and then worked as a journalist. She became well-known after the publication of her first novel, "Nectar In A Sieve" (1954), which became an international bestseller, and which was followed by nine other novels. All of Markandaya's novels display her deep preoccupation with changing Indian society and politics. "Nectar In A Sieve" was translated into more than a dozen languages. It is a moving story of peasant India, in which the weather conditions as well as the winds of change are stoically borne by the poor landless farmers. Together with her second most popular novel, "A Handful Of Rice" (1966), "Nectar In A Sieve" was and still is being taught in literature courses both in public schools and universities in America.*

Lernwortschatz *fail, grain, to weep, compassion, to comfort, to scan, serenity, faint, spark, obstinate, to scour for sth., to shrink, shoot, stain, to choke, to reap, heap, drought, fissure, to creep, to perish, prone, to gasp, greed, spite, to decree, to shrivel, seed, to sprout, tender, to thrust, slender, spire, to rustle, to tug, peasant, to engulf, to falter, to ripen, to wither, prosperous, to roam, gutter, plight, edible, to retch, to devour, sequel, dull, to assail, limb, to retain, to stifle*

Materialien → **Online-Link: 601006-0012**

Der Text wird zunächst einmal im Plenum gelesen oder er wird von den S bereits zu Hause erarbeitet. Hinweis auf die *Fact file* zu *The monsoon* und die *VIP file* zu Kamala Markandaya.

Evaluation

1 *Create a diagram or flow chart showing how…*

Aufgabe 1 wird in Partnerarbeit oder in Kleingruppen erledigt. Ggf erhalten einzelne S eine Folie, auf der sie ihre *flow charts* oder Diagramme schreiben, die sie dann dem Plenum präsentieren.

Lösungsvorschlag **a)** *Flow chart, see p. 47.*

b) *Both husband and wife try to comfort each other by stressing that the time of the harvest will soon come. The first-person narrator suppresses the question of whether they will have enough strength to be alive when the time has come. The exchange is similar to the sentence "Perhaps tomorrow" which Nathan says at the beginning of the text and which indicates the glimmer of hope that he and the other villagers have that the rain will come in the end. As their hopes are dashed, however, the reader is left with the impression at the end of the text that there might be another drought and the vicious circle will not be broken.*

Flow chart

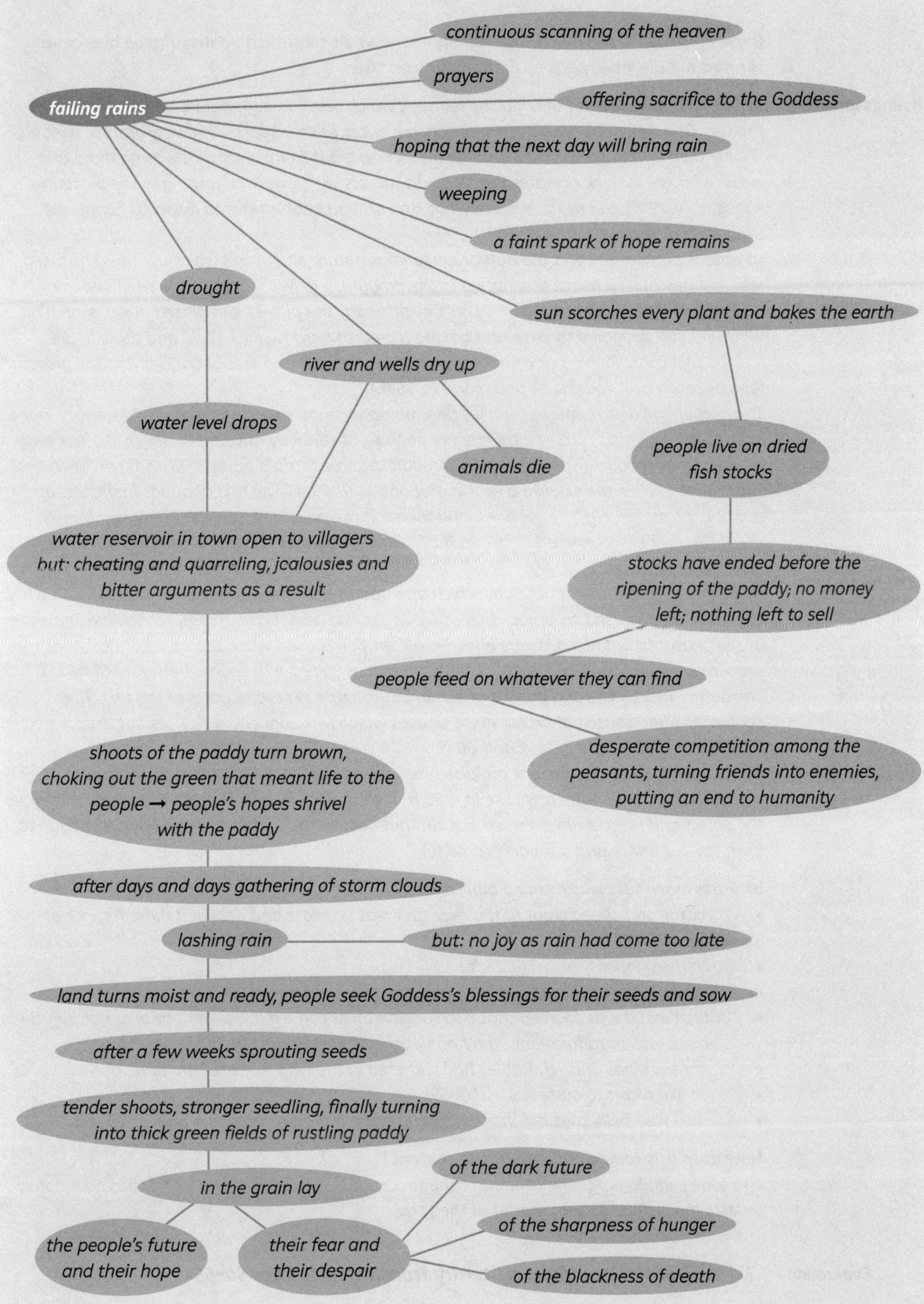

Result – hunger: *first a prevalent condition, a gnawing pain; after eating something hunger turns from a sharp into a dull pain; one cannot avoid the thought however hard one tries; finally, however, all the pain and all the desire are gone, replaced by great emptiness and an overwhelming weakness*

Analysis

2 *Analyse how the author achieves such intensity in the style of the text.*

Diese Aufgabe wird in einer Stillarbeitsphase oder als schriftliche **Hausaufgabe** bearbeitet. Hinweis auf die *Word bank* zu *Commenting on style.*

Lösungsvorschlag

a) *The author uses a set of linguistic features which result in a great intensity in the style of the text. She describes the effects and consequences of the drought in a very graphic way, e.g. "Plants died and the grass rotted, cattle and sheep crept to the river that was no more and perished there for lack of water, lizards and squirrels lay prone and gasping in the blistering sunlight" (ll. 22 ff). Her description of what kind of food people have to resort to during the drought is also very graphic (ll. 60 ff).*
In various parts of the text the author personifies nature and in this way illustrates the merciless and destructive forces originating in the drought, e.g. "We stared at the cruel sky, calm, blue, indifferent to our need" (ll. 1–2) or "Day after day the pitiless sun blazed down, scorching whatever still struggled to grow and baking the earth hard [...]" (ll. 19 ff.) and then, finally "... the rain came lashing down, making up in fury for the long drought and giving the grateful land as much as it could suck and more" (ll. 36 ff.).
The author employs numerous similes and metaphors and thus also creates an intensity in the style of the text, e.g. "... only a faint spark of hope, obstinately refusing to die" (l. 11), "the well was as dry as a bone" (l. 14), "the stain spread like some terrible disease" (ll. 15 ff.) or "Then that too is gone ..., like the sky, like a well in drought ... (ll. 79 ff). The text abounds in archaic and poetic expressions, e.g. "... not one cloud to mar its serenity" (l. 8); "... and perished there" (l. 23), "So thither I journeyed ..." (ll. 26 ff.), "... in like plight to ourselves" (l. 66), or "A terrible sickness assails you ..." (l. 77).
Some passages contain repetitions which also add to the intensive style, e.g in ll. 50–55 in which the noun "fear" is used six times, thus conveying to the reader a very comprehensible impression of the peasants' emotions. A very effective alliteration is used when the narrator describes the seedlings, which "stood out singly, slender, tremulous spires with spaces between" (ll. 46 ff.).
The author makes use of a particular sentence structure in several parts of the text. The sentences often consist of two or more clauses which lack connective devices but are connected by commas only (e.g. in ll. 22 ff. or ll. 60 ff.).
Present participle constructions are also often used (e.g. l. 16, l. 63, l. 72). The author also employs many enumerations with "and", like in ll. 30 ff., ll. 41 ff., ll. 45 ff., ll. 74 ff., ll. 80 ff. In many sentences the object and subject are reversed, e.g. "In that field, in the grain which had not yet begun to form, lay our future and our hope" (ll. 48 ff.).

b) ***Parts in the text which sound biblical***
- *"..., cattle and sheep crept to the river that was no more and perished there for lack of water, ..." (ll. 22 ff.)*
- *"So thither I journeyed ..." (ll. 26 ff.)*
- *"..., and there were jealousies and spite and bitter argument." (ll. 30 ff.)*
- *"Until at last it was decreed that each person must come in his own right only, not for others, ...; but it was hard for many who had not their full strength." (ll. 31 ff.)*
- *"..., for the vines and vegetables had withered in the long weeks of drought." (ll. 58 ff.)*
- *"..., in like plight to ourselves, ..." (l. 66)*
- *"..., and your belly cries out insistently, and there is a gnawing and a pain ..." (l. 73)*

How does this tone complement the content?
This tone complements the content of the text, as it is solemn and grave and thus adequately reflects the serious subject matter of the text.

Evaluation

3 [👥] *Translation: Make a literary translation of lines 50–55.*

Die Übersetzung wird am besten als **Hausaufgabe** angefertigt. Die Ergebnisse können dann in der folgenden Unterrichtsstunde mit dem Nachbarn verglichen und diskutiert werden.

Lösungsvorschlag

Hoffnung und Angst. Untrennbare Kräfte, die uns zunächst in die eine und dann in die andere Richtung zogen; welche der beiden die stärkere Kraft war, konnte niemand sagen. Von letzterer sprachen wir niemals, aber sie war immer bei uns. Angst, ständiger Begleiter des Kleinbauern. Hunger, sich immer wieder ins Gedächtnis rufend, wenn er einmal nachlassen sollte. Verzweiflung, bereit, ihn zu verschlingen, wenn er einmal stocken sollte. Angst; Angst vor der düsteren Zukunft; Angst vor der Heftigkeit des Hungers; Angst vor der Schwärze des Todes.

Novel excerpt

The Solitude of Emperors

pp. 32–33

HINTERGRUNDINFO

David Davidar*, who was born in 1959 in Kerala, is an author and publisher. In his mid-twenties, he moved to Bombay to pursue journalism, before turning to publishing and obtaining a diploma in publishing from Harvard University. He became head of Penguin India in 1985, boosting the number of publications from a mere six titles in 1987 to 150 titles per year. In 2004 he transferred to Penguin Canada. David Davidar has written two novels so far; his later one, "The Solitude of Emperors", was published in 2007 and was shortlisted for the Commonwealth Writers' Prize.*

Lernwortschatz *to contribute, disenchantment, a lack of opportunity, slow pace, petty, jealousy, concern, to associate with sb, desperation, economics, ambition, to advance, career, previous, succeeding, achievement, to attend, intention, to disown, progressiveness, to extend, to scheme, to endure, to sneak, to aid, escape, charitable, tension, to deplete, to get by, to come round, to assure, to raise a child, to intend to do sth, to forgive, occasion, modest, reconciliation, as a result, memory, to possess, humiliation, to exacerbate, to dilute, to linger, to delete, to inherit, stubbornness, temper, to blame sb for sth, to fulfil a promise, token, gesture, to hang out with sb (infml), to impose sth on sb, faith, to tolerate, to face sth, numerous, indignity, to dwell on sth, alienation, to take one's toll, dense, humidity, charms, to reveal, to scale down one's expectations*

Als Einstieg diskutieren die S, inwiefern sich das Leben in ländlichen Gebieten Indiens wohl vom Leben in indischen Großstädten unterscheidet. Nach der Lektüre des Textes erfolgt die Bearbeitung der beiden Fragen, die entweder schriftlich oder in der Diskussion im Plenum erfolgen kann.

Comprehension

1 *Sum up the story of Vijay's parents …*

Die Zusammenfassung kann als schriftliche **Hausaufgabe** erfolgen. Hinweis auf die *VIP file* zu David Davidar.

Lösungsvorschlag *Vijay's parents belong to different castes, which usually would have made it impossible for them to get married. Vijay's father belonged to the Brahmin caste and his mother was a member of the Chettiar caste. However, against all odds they secretly married in 1967 in the small town of Salem, where they both had grown up. His mother and father had both attended the same college where they had met and fallen in love. Both sets of parents did not accept their wish to get married – Vijay's grandfather disowned his son whereas Vijay's mother was locked up in her room and beaten by her father for three days. Her parents were planning to send her to a distant relative. However, Vijay's mother managed to escape and after their secret marriage the couple soon left their hometown for K- where they spent the rest of their lives. Vijay's father was eventually reconciled with his family, whereas his mother's father remained irreconcilable.*
Vijay characterises his parents as quite content with their careers as lecturers of physics and economics, respectively, at two colleges in Vijay's hometown K-. He says that they did not display any form of ambition or guile to get ahead in their careers (l. 8) He muses about the reasons for this attitude and suggests that they did not have any "real expectations in life", as they were "part of the generation of Indians born on the cusp of independence" (ll. 10 ff.), who, in contrast to the generation before them, did not really have any serious issues to struggle for. He also attributes their lack of zest to the turmoil in the first phase of their romance and argues that they might have been happy at having overcome those difficulties and subsequently savoured a calm life (ll. 30 ff.).

Analysis

2 *Compare the ways Vijay presents his hometown K- on the one hand ...*

Die Diskussion erfolgt am besten im Plenum. Hinweis auf den Tipp zu *Bombay, Calcutta* und *Madras*.

Lösungsvorschlag

Vijay did not feel accepted in his hometown K-. Religion and caste were the two predominant issues that the lives of most families revolved around. Vijay's parents had crossed caste lines and despite the fact that his father had promised Vijay's grandfather that he would raise his son to be a good Brahmin, he did not do so. This marked him out "as an oddity, a mongrel" (l. 44). Both his parents had turned their back on religion and thus Vijay "grew up without religion" (l. 58). As at school and in college the boys mixed mainly with boys of their own caste and religion, Vijay felt like a social outcast who was tolerated to some degree but not really integrated. This deepened his "sense of alienation" (l. 70).

Vijay wanted to leave his hometown as he considered the big cities to be more tolerant. He had heard that there "you could do as you pleased, marry who you liked, go wherever you wanted" (ll. 71–72). Right from the first moments that he spent in Bombay, he felt at home and at ease with the people there: "These were my people, I thought; I was a Bombayite now" (ll. 84–85). However, in the course of time he noticed that his expectations could not be met and that "Bombay's sense of possibility and adventure was largely an illusion" (ll. 86–87). However, he is still thrilled by the city and its vibrant atmosphere despite the functional architecture, the salty air, "the slums, noise, dense crowds, humidity, crime and pollution" (l. 76).

Interview transcript/Video clip

A shocking transformation

pp. 34–35

Lernwortschatz *transformation, literally, income, to come about, prosperity, to bring sth home to sb, deprivation, to be distressed, engrained, approach, to acquire, soluble (fml), sustainable, to rid sth of sth, confident, famine, likelihood, to tackle*

Materialien → **Online-Link: 601006-0013**

Die S stellen zunächst Vermutungen zum Inhalt des Interviews an. L: *The text is a transcript of an interview on the changes that have taken place in India in the last couple of years. What are your expectations regarding the contents of the text, particularly if you take into consideration the title "A shocking transformation" and if you have a look at the photographs?* Nachdem die S ihre Vermutungen verbalisiert haben, wird der Text zunächst einmal gemeinsam gelesen.

Analysis

1 *Outline what the text says about: 1. the changes that have taken place ...*

Aufgabe 1 eignet sich als Partner- oder Einzelarbeit. Hinweis auf die Wendungen in der *Word bank*.

Lösungsvorschlag

a) 1. *The changes that have taken place in India*

Industrial parks and American-style shopping malls selling western labels are spreading in the cities, taking over huge areas of land. A new middle class with a large disposable income has emerged. People no longer aspire to a professional career as a doctor, lawyer or accountant but want to get a job in the new technologies which have become so important in India's economy. At the same time a new class of super-rich Indians, i.e. "huge numbers of millionaires and billionaires" (ll. 24 ff.) has been created, a fact which makes the huge gulf between the wealthy and the poor even more obvious.

2. *The reasons that lie behind these changes*

India's new economy focuses on information technology and there is a rising importance of the financial services and the service industries. These sectors rely heavily on the middle class, as "the Indian boom has been very middle-class-knowledge-driven" (ll. 12 ff.). Thus the members of the middle-class have gained a large disposable income. The economy has also enabled individuals with an ordinary upbringing to earn incredible sums of money within a comparatively short period of time.

3. ***The Indian attitude towards wealth***
Indians consider attaining prosperity as entirely positive, as "there is no guilt associated with being wealthy" (l. 39). The Hindu religion promotes this attitude as it "encourages people to acquire wealth as part of their lives" (l. 43). There is also the belief that it's better to focus on one's own advancement than bothering "about the beggar or the guy who's living on the street, or the way your servant lives" (ll. 35 ff.).

b) *Krishnan Guru-Marthy is of the opinion that hundreds of millions of Indians need to transform their way of life. Small farms of two or three acres need to be replaced by more profitable, bigger farms and thus a huge number of peasants will have to change their jobs (ll. 49–54). He thinks that the best case scenario for India would be to turn into one of the top three economies of the world which will begin to assert its political role in the world, too. He then expresses his fear that the new economy will not affect the whole country and thus hundreds of millions of Indians in the country will be unemployed and without any land. These people would be totally excluded from the economic success of the country and be "shut out of the new India" (l. 76). Krishnan Guru-Marthy does not believe that this development would lead to a revolution but he asserts that this fundamental problem must be tackled in order to prevent social chaos.*

Analysis

2 [4] *Watch the video and compare the different perspectives ...*

Materialien → **Film 4 (Migration to the cities)**

[4] Der Videoclip wird zweimal vorgespielt, wobei sich die S Notizen zu den in Aufgabe **a)** vorgegebenen Aspekten machen. Im Anschluss werden die Ergebnisse im Plenum besprochen. Teilaufgabe **b)** eignet sich als Partnerarbeit oder als Aufgabe für Kleingruppen.

Lösungsvorschlag

a) *People leave their villages because there are no jobs for them in rural India. They hope to find employment in the cities. However, this mass migration puts a serious strain on the infrastructure of these cities, e.g. Mumbai. There is also fierce competition in the job market which results in dangerous resentment among city dwellers. Some of those believe that the migrants bring filth with them and that they don't care about their surroundings. They want them to leave their city. Migrants often end up with poorly-paid work and long hours as well as poor housing. There are, however, some success stories. For some migrants the city has offered opportunities and they have advanced and can now provide a living for their families.*

b) ***Dangers of mass migration to the cities***
- *serious strain on the education system, health facilities, power and water supplies in the big cities; worst case scenario: collapse of the infrastructure*
- *fierce competition in the job market*
- *evolving slums with poor housing and bad sanitation, which might eventually lead to urban decay and social unrest*
- *impending social problems as migrants leave behind deep-rooted traditions and family ties*

Possibilities of mass migration to the cities
- *a demand for houses, office buildings, shopping centres and other facilities from the rural masses might instigate a building boom and a further advancement of the economy in India*
- *the new urban migrants might further improve India's emerging information technology sector, its service sector as well as its financial services as these migrants are ambitious and keen on making a career for themselves*
- *thus a shift in the labour force from the agricultural sector to the urbanised economy might lead to decreasing poverty for millions of Indians*

Evaluation

3 *Creative writing: Imagine the future of India and write an article ...*

Zusatzmaterial → **Klausurvorschlag 3 • Revision file 3**

Den Artikel arbeiten die S am besten als schriftliche **Hausaufgabe** aus.

Lösungsvorschlag ***India in the year 2050 – a best case scenario***

Evolving from the India of the mid-20th century which was a poor developing country, India has become one of the most important economic superpowers in the world, second only to America and China. Its population is over 1.5 billion. Due to the incredible ambition and skills of this large, young and educated population, it has attained a very prominent place in the globalised world of the 21st century and has successfully reached a vital place on the world's political stage. India's stable democratic system of government has been able to tackle all the challenges that the rising population and the incredibly fast development of its economy have instigated. At the beginning of the millennium considerable investments in health care and education took place. A decade later the government focused primarily on the development of renewable energy sources (biomass, solar and wind), technologies and infrastructure to meet an increasing shortage in energy.

Thus India has been able to solve one of the most fundamental problems it faced only 40 years ago when despite increased wealth and a burgeoning urban middle class, the vast majority of India's rural population remained illiterate and impoverished. Today people in the country lead a comfortable life as farming methods have been improved to the effect that farmers are no longer dependent on favourable weather conditions. Seasonal water scarcity is successfully tackled by intricate irrigation systems throughout the country. India has an urban population of around six hundred million, more than twice as high as in 2001. Old two-storey houses have been replaced by buildings four-storeys or higher. Old factory land has been turned into multi-storey office buildings, commercial and residential spaces. City governments have worked hard for the last couple of decades to optimise the infrastructure with the result that there have never been any instances of water shortages, the collapse of public transportation, a threat to the health care system or similar problems within the last 20 years. Because of the increasing wealth and comfortable living condition for all Indians, old barriers of gender, religion and caste have broken down so that equality has been reached.

Erweiterung Zum Abschluss des *Topics* füllen die S *Revision file* 3 (Themenheft, Seite 62) aus. Ein Lösungsvorschlag befindet sich hier im Lehrerheft (Seite 111).

Topic 4: East meets West

pp. 36–49

Didaktisches Inhaltsverzeichnis

Bearbeitungszeitraum: 12–14 Unterrichtsstunden

Textsorte / Thema	Unterrichts-methoden	*Input boxes*	Kompetenzen	Textproduktion
India's magic works wonders!, 2005 (340 words)				SB, Seite 36/37, LB, Seite 54–57
Combination of visuals, cartoon, Internet article/The fascination of India	Kursgespräch Online-Link: 601006-0014 Zusatzmaterial: Kopiervorlage 8	*Word banks*	Orientierungswissen Bildbeschreibung/ -analyse Leseverstehen Gespräche führen	*Describing and comparing pictures* *Summarising aspects* *Discussing advantages and disadvantages* *Analysing a cartoon*
A family of Anglophiles, 1997 (1070 words)				SB, Seite 38/39, LB, Seite 57–59
Novel excerpt/ Anglophiles in India	Kursgespräch Online-Link: 601006-0015 Zusatzmaterial: Kopiervorlage 9	*Fact file: British influence in India* *VIP file: Arundhati Roy* *Word bank*	Leseverstehen Hör-/Sehverstehen Gespräche führen Argumentieren Recherchieren	*Analysing characters* *Commenting on aspects*
[5] **The world as India, 2007** (807 words)				SB, Seite 40/41, LB, Seite 59–62
Essay excerpt, cartoon, video clip/ Information technology in India	Kursgespräch Gruppenarbeit Online-Link: 601006-0016	*VIP file: Susan Sontag* *Word bank: International business*	Orientierungswissen Leseverstehen Bildbeschreibung/ -analyse Hör-/Sehverstehen Gespräche führen Argumentieren	*Summarising developments* *Comparing the pros and cons* *Taking notes* *Acting out a discussion*
[5] **The Gateway of India, 2007** (966 words)				SB, Seite 42/43, LB, Seite 63–65
Novella excerpt/ A business trip to India	Kursgespräch Online-Link: 601006-0017	*VIP file: Paul Theroux* *Word bank*	Leseverstehen Hörverstehen Gespräche führen Recherchieren	*Describing a character* *Writing a dialogue* *Writing an article for a travel guide*
Fashion's dirty secret/Träume in Pink, Gold, Orange, 2006 (532/423 words)				SB, Seite 44/45, LB, Seite 65–67
Newspaper articles/ Child labour in India, Bollywood	Kursgespräch Online-Link: 601006-0018	*Word bank: Letter to the editor*	Leseverstehen Gespräche führen Hör-/Sehverstehen Mediation	*Describing aspects* *Writing a letter to the editor* *Summing up information*
[6] **Jasmine, 1989** (1005 words)				SB, Seite 46/47, LB, Seite 67–69
Novel excerpt/ Immigrant experiences	Kursgespräch Online-Link: 601006-0019	*VIP file: Bharati Mukherjee*	*Leseverstehen* *Hörverstehen* *Gespräche führen* *Argumentieren*	*Summing up facts* *Pointing out details* *Analysing the narrative perspective*
[7] **The Mistress of Spices, 1997** (916 words)				SB, Seite 48/49, LB, Seite 69–72
Novel excerpt/ Immigrant experiences	Kursgespräch Online-Link: 601006-0020 Zusatzmaterial: Klausurvorschlag 4	*Fact file: The Ramayana* *VIP file: Chitra Banerjee Divakaruni*	*Leseverstehen* *Hörverstehen* *Gespräche führen* *Argumentieren*	*Taking notes* *Describing and interpreting aspects* *Analysing the style* *Comparing and contrasting texts*

Unterrichtsverlauf

Photographs/ Cartoon/Internet article

India's magic works wonders! pp. 36–37

Lernwortschatz *tie, voyage, treasure, deserve, alumnus, aside from (mainly AE), to flock to sth, to impact, sensuality*

Materialien → **Online-Link: 601006-0014**

Die Auftaktdoppelseite bietet den Hintergrund für eine vertiefte Auseinandersetzung der S mit der wechselseitigen Befruchtung der westlichen Welt und Indiens in kultureller, wirtschaftlicher und kulinarischer Hinsicht.

Comprehension

1 *Explain the idea expressed in the text ...*

Die Fragestellungen werden im Plenum oder alternativ in Kleingruppen besprochen.

Lösungsvorschlag

a) *Centuries ago Western powers came to the orient as colonists and ruled various countries for a considerable time. Today, too, Westerners come to the East and look for "modern treasures" (l. 5). Whereas Columbus was looking for goods like spices or other valuable materials in India, Westerners today are searching for less tangible things such as attitudes and concepts, knowledge, ideas, art or services (ll. 6–7, ll. 25–26). Thus the contact between East and West has come full circle.*

b) *In the US Indian-born men and women have attained top positions in several areas, e.g. in "education, business, research, fashion and art" (ll. 10 ff). Moreover, Bollywood film productions as well as literature written by Indian authors have made a great mark on the West. The West is also considerably influenced by Indian fashion, lifestyle, weddings and jewellery as well as art (ll. 18–23). Other "goods" which are being exported to the West from India are "abstract qualities like exoticism and sensuality" (l. 26).*

Aspects pupils might mention as evidence of this in Germany

- *the pervasiveness of Asian takeaways or restaurants in cities*
- *the demand for Indian-style goods like carpets or furnishings as well as accessories and attire*
- *the interest of viewers in films from and about India (Slumdog Millionaire was shown in huge cinemas for several weeks and has sold quite well on DVD)*
- *the enthusiasm of a considerable number of people in Germany for yoga*
- *the fact that ayurveda products as well as courses of treatment based on ayurveda have gained a remarkable share of the market*

Discussion

2 *From what you have learned both about India's history ...*

Die Aufgaben werden zunächst in Partnerarbeit vorbereitet und dann im Plenum diskutiert. Hinweis auf die *Word bank*.

Lösungsvorschlag

a)

- *In the late nineteenth and early twentieth centuries, Indians moved to the West as migrant workers who toiled in factories, mills or as agricultural labourers in the US or Britain, for example.*
- *These people were looking for a better life and the end of suppression or discrimination by the British (cf. the belief in the United States as "The Land of the Free" and "The Land of Opportunity" or in Britain as the mother country of democracy) and the caste system.*
- *Until the Commonwealth Immigrants Act 1962, immigration to Britain was quite easy, since all British Empire and Commonwealth citizens were allowed to enter and stay in the United Kingdom without any restriction because they carried a British passport.*
- *After India became independent in 1947, there was another wave of immigration: professionals and skilled workers moved to the industrially advanced countries like the*

United States, England and Canada in search for good career opportunities. And the rich people sent their children to schools and universities in the West.

- *Today many peasants, menial workers as well as street traders or petty tradesmen leave their country in order to find better chances in the economies of the West.*

b) ***Possible advantages***

- *India's image has changed because of the success and expertise of Indians abroad: India now is associated with brain power, high tech and particularly IT solutions and software development.*
- *In particular the Indian nationality of software programmers working in Silicon Valley or with computer and software firms in Germany like SAP or Dell enhances India's reputation as an IT specialist country.*
- *Foreign-trained Indians are starting their own businesses in India, thus making use of their acquired skills and knowledge and contributing to India's economic boom.*
- *Moreover, foreign companies are expanding their offices in India, and they are hiring foreign-trained workers who are interested in returning to India.*
- *These entrepreneurs as well as foreign companies and investors who rely on the skills of former emigrants accelerate economic development in India.*

Possible disadvantages

- *Due to mass emigration, India has lost millions of highly skilled, well-educated or professional people, which has not contributed to the development of India's economy, health care and education systems, arts and culture etc.*
- *Thus India has lost the knowledge, skills, work as well as the taxes of these mostly young emigrants.*
- *Although India has great human resources, more developed countries have thus profited from India's best minds.*

Brainteaser

3 Share what you know about ayurveda and yoga, ...

Die S machen sich zunächst in einer Stillarbeitsphase Notizen zu den verschiedenen Aspekten und tauschen dann in einer Diskussion im Kurs ihre Kenntnisse zu **a)** und ihre persönlichen Ansichten zu **b)** aus. Hinweis auf die *Word bank*.

Lösungsvorschlag

a) *Individual answers.*

b) ***Possible aspects students could mention***

- *Asia has always been fascinating for Europeans, as early as the time of Marco Polo, for example.*
- *India in particular had and still has the lure of the exotic with its different religions, its diverse traditions, its lush colours, its music, its spices, etc.; this otherness is in stark contrast to western cultures.*
- *Some people might hope that by devoting themselves to Indian philosophy and its core ideals they might be able to leave behind the negative impacts that the Western way of life has on them. They might search for an alternative to the consumerism, the competition, the pressure, etc. that they associate with the West.*
- *Some people might be fascinated by the holistic tendencies of Indian ideas, e.g. ayurveda.*
- *Westerners might be attracted to the more mystical and exotic sides of Indian religion and thus try to apply these traditions to their own life by practising meditation and yoga, for example.*

Analysis

4 Analyse and interpret the cartoon.

Zusatzmaterial

→ **Kopiervorlage 8 a/b (Analysing cartoons – Part I/II)**

Diese Aufgabe wird als schriftliche **Hausaufgabe** angefertigt.

Lösungsvorschlag

In my opinion the cartoon pokes fun at some westerners' tendency to consider Indian philosophy uncritically as a way of expanding one's mind and receiving helpful advice for one's

life. The cartoon depicts an old, balding man with a long white beard, clad only in a loin-cloth, sitting cross-legged on top of a mountain. In the background you can see several snow-covered mountain tops. In the foreground two mountaineers are shown. In the bottom right-hand corner only the head of the mountaineer can be seen. The old man is talking to the other mountaineer, who is looking up at him, obviously in awe. The old man, however, is giving the man, presumably a westerner, a look of incredulity. The caption says: "You've come all this way seeking great wisdom, from someone who's stupid enough to sit half naked on top of a mountain?"
The cartoon ridicules the uncritical attitude of some westerners towards Indian philosophy and Indian gurus. The cartoonist hints at the fact that some westerners spare no trouble in order to seek guidance from Indian philosophical leaders or teachers but do not realise that they might only be fascinated by that school of thinking because it is so different and exotic in comparison with western philosophy.

Erweiterung Die **Kopiervorlagen 8 a/b** (Seite 85/86) enthalten die wesentlichen Schritte zur Beschreibung und Interpretation eines Cartoons und bieten eine Liste mit Wendungen, die die S für die Analyse eines Cartoons verwenden können. Die S interpretieren einen Cartoon schriftlich.

Evaluation

5 [💻] *Research: Find out about one of the successful Indians ...*

Die S recherchieren zu Hause im Internet Hintergrundinformationen zu einer (oder zwei) der genannten Persönlichkeiten und stellen ihre Ergebnisse in einer kurzen Präsentation dem Plenum vor.

Lösungsvorschlag

Indira Nuyi (Nooyi)

- *Nuyi was born in India in 1955.*
- *She studied chemistry and management in India and received a Master's degree in Management at Yale University, USA.*
- *She then worked for the Boston Consulting Group, Motorola and Asea Brown Boveri before she joined PepsiCo, one of the world's leading food and beverage companies, in 1994.*
- *She became Chief Executive Officer (CEO) of PepsiCo in 2006 and the Chairperson of the company in 2007.*
- *Indira Nuyi was listed among Time's 100 most influential people in the world in 2007 and 2008 and reached top positions in various lists of most influential business leaders published by renowned magazines like Forbes or Fortune.*

Srinija Srinivasan

- *Srinivasan is vice-president and editor-in-chief of Yahoo!; she is responsible for the design and maintenance of Yahoo!'s overall classification and organisation scheme.*
- *Born in India, she came to the US at three months and she spent her childhood as a south Indian Brahman in Lawrence, Kansas.*
- *She studied at the university of Stanford where she received a bachelor's degree in Symbolic Systems.*
- *In 1992 she spent an internship in Japan. At Kyoto campus she met and befriended David Filo und Jerry Yang, two Standford graduate students who in 1995 founded Yahoo!.*
- *She was employed by Filo and Yang as the company's fifth employee and created the basic structure of the Yahoo directory in 1995.*
- *Newsweek listed her as one of the 50 people who matter most on the Internet (Dec 25, 1995).*
- *Srinija Srinivasan was instrumental in building the start-up company into a $30 billion corporation with roughly 2.1 billion page views a day.*

Padmasree Warrior

- *Warrior was born and raised in in the southern state of Andhra Pradesh, India.*
- *She studied chemical engineering in Delhi (bachelor's degree) and received her masters degree from Cornell University, USA.*
- *In 1984 she was employed by Motorola, where she held various positions in the years following before she became the CTO (Chief Technology Officer) of the company in 2003, being the first female executive of the corporation.*
- *Padmasree Warrior is now the CTO of Cisco Systems, a position she has held since 2007.*

Srikant M. Datar

- *After graduating from the University of Bombay he received two master's degrees and a Ph.D. from Stanford University.*
- *In 2009 Dr. Datar was appointed to the Board of Directors of Stryker Corporation, a medical technology company.*
- *He serves as Senior Associate Dean and Director of Research at the Graduate School of Business Administration of Harvard University, USA.*
- *He has also held the Arthur Lowes Dickinson Professorship of Accounting at Harvard University since 1996.*

Salman Rushdie

- *Sir Ahmed Salman Rushdie is a British Indian novelist and essayist who was born in Mumbai in 1947.*
- *He attended school in Mumbai as well as at Rugby in England.*
- *After graduation from King's College, Cambridge, where he had studied history, he briefly lived in Pakistan where his family had moved before he returned to England and worked as a copywriter for an advertising agency.*
- *Salman Rushdie became famous after the publication of his second novel, the acclaimed "Midnight's Children", which won the Booker Prize in 1981.*
- *The publication of his fourth novel, "The Satanic Verses", in 1988 caused protests from Muslims in several countries who accused Rushdie of blasphemy against Islam.*
- *Ayatollah Ruhollah Khomeini, the Supreme Leader of Iran, issued a fatwa against Rushdie in 1989; as this was effectively a sentence of death, Rushdie was forced into hiding, remaining under the protection of the British government and police.*
- *Salman Rushdie has continued to write and publish books; his latest novel, "The Enchantress of Florence", was published in 2008.*
- *In 2007 Queen Elizabeth II appointed him a Knight Bachelor for "services to literature".*

Vikram Chandra

- *Chandra was born in India in 1961 and as an undergraduate student moved to the United States where he studied English with a focus on creative writing.*
- *In 1987 he received his M.A. from The Writing Seminars at Johns Hopkins University in Baltimore, Maryland.*
- *He is an acclaimed writer of novels and short stories who has received various awards for his literary work.*
- *Chandra also teaches creative writing at the University of California, Berkeley.*

Novel excerpt

A family of Anglophiles

pp. 38–39

HINTERGRUNDINFO

Suzanna Arundhati Roy, *who was born in Kerala, India, in 1961 to a Keralite Christian mother and a Bengali Hindu father, is an acclaimed Indian writer who received the Booker Prize for her first novel, "The God of Small Things", in 1997. Roy is also a political and social activist who is strongly associated with the anti-globalisation movement as well as a staunch critic of neo-imperialism. Arundhati Roy trained as an architect at the School of Architecture and Planning in New Delhi, where she met her first husband Gerald DaCunha. She abandoned architecture, however, and became better known for her complex, scathing film scripts. Roy also appeared as a performer in some films, e.g. in "In Which Annie Gives It Those Ones" (1989), a film directed by her second husband, Pradip Krishen.*

With the publication of "The God of Small Things" Arundhati Roy received international acclaim and fame. The novel, which became an international best-seller, received numerous positive reviews, but also caused controversy and criticism. Roy, for instance, had to answer charges of obscenity in her homestate Kerala, as the Chief Minister there accused her of unrestrained description of sexuality. Roy has concentrated her writing on political issues since the publication of her first novel. She has written on varied topics such as India's nuclear weapons, the Narmada Dam project, and American power giant Enron's activities in India.

*For **Jawaharlal Nehru** see* **Hintergrundinfo***, p. 40.*

Lernwortschatz *tin, to distribute, dowry, to be thrilled, affection, incurable, to be well disposed to sb/sth, to demolish, trapped, to retrace, extensive, litigation, dim, plump, translucent, to crumble, to gossip, to invade, to capture, to adore sb/sth, to despise sb/sth, to refer to, contempt, to scorn, to disdain, ashore, sorely, awe, to humble, contemporary, ceiling*

Materialien → **Online-Link: 601006-0015**

Der Text wird zunächst einmal im Plenum gelesen oder er wird von den S bereits zu Hause erarbeitet. Hinweis auf die *Fact file* zu Jawaharlal Nehru und die *VIP file* zu Arundhati Roy.

Analysis

1 *Examine how Chacko is characterised. How do references to other ...?*

Die S erledigen die Aufgabe in Stillarbeit oder in Partnerarbeit.

Lösungsvorschlag *Chacko is predominantly characterised in an indirect way, i.e. the significant traits of his character are shown through what he says and does. At the end of this extract, there are instances of direct characterisation, too, as the author, through her narrator and through the remarks of another character in the story, i.e. Ammu, Chacko's wife, mentions some of Chacko's qualities directly.*

Chacko seems to be a very strong-minded man, who is not easily influenced by what other people think or say. This particularly becomes obvious in two passages in the text; first, when he talks about his father being an Anglophile and thus refuting what his sister Ammu had said about him being an "incurable British CCP" or "shit-sweeper" (ll. 10 ff.). Second, when he is lecturing to his young nephew and niece about the state of mind of the Indian people and totally ignores his sister's comment, which is obviously intended as a personal insult or criticism directed at Chacko (ll. 44–51). He obviously feels superior to his sister as he does not really pay attention to what she says. He also treats her children in a condescending way, lecturing about high-flown ideas and making them look up difficult words in a dictionary. He is seemingly a rather pedantic man, as he insists on the children looking up the exact definitions of difficult words and phrases. He obviously overtaxes these children and keeps talking over their head, but neither their mother nor they themselves seem to shun his company. When Chacko is in this talkative mood and relentlessly displays his oratory style, he "didn't care whether anyone was listening to him or not. And if they were, he didn't care whether or not they had understood what he was saying" (ll. 81 ff.), which his sister describes as "his Oxford Moods" (l. 83), hinting at the fact that her brother was educated at Oxford University.

Comprehension

2 *Explain Chacko's view of the effect of being a family of Anglophiles and ...*

Zusatzmaterial → **Kopiervorlage 9 (Vocabulary work)**

Diese Aufgabe eignet sich als schriftliche **Hausaufgabe**. Hinweis auf die *Word bank.*

Lösungsvorschlag **a)** *Chacko regrets having to say that his family is a family of Anglophiles (ll. 21–22). He believes that this means being irrevocably separated from one's own history and not being able to "retrace their steps because their footprints had been swept away" (ll. 23–24). This implies that the British have taken away his family's roots and their freedom to move, an idea which is taken up again in the extended simile of history being an old house they have been shut out of (ll. 44–58). Chacko is convinced that being deprived of their cultural identitiy they are like prisoners, and as their lives as well as their wishes, hopes, feelings and dreams are irrelevant, they will never be able to gain positions of power in either of the two worlds (ll. 55–58).*

b) *I think the extended simile "history is like an old house at night" that Chacko uses is a suitable comparison as it emphasises that one really has to make an effort and find out more about the past in order to understand history. Chacko believes that everyone should be able to go inside the house and listen, look and smell for themselves, but by using the metaphors "shadows" and "whispering" he points out that it will never be possible for people who are disconnected from their roots (= "locked out") to see, hear or understand fully what happened in the past and how everything is connected. According to him, the people who are not entirely* *part of a culture but caught between different ones are denied the real experience of history (ll. 25–28).*

Other similes

History is like a difficult book. It contains facts and figures which are not comprehensible to all. Some aspects are open to interpretation; others might be biased or even manipulated. Thus every reader draws different conclusions. Not even real experts can fully understand it.
History is like a wise old man. He keeps telling us interesting, amazing, overwhelming, saddening, depressing or frightening stories. He keeps reminding us to lead a good and moral life. He keeps telling us what went wrong in his life. He keeps warning us not to repeat his own mistakes. We sometimes listen, we sometimes ridicule, we sometimes ignore him.

Erweiterung

- ***Metaphors focusing on history – food for thought***
  "History is a cyclic poem written by Time upon the memories of man." (Percy Bysshe Shelley)
  "History is philosophy teaching by examples." (Thucydides, The History of the Peloponnesian War)
  "History is a mighty dramos, enacted upon the theatre of times, with suns for lamps and eternity for a background." (Thomas Carlyle)
  "History is the sum total of the things that could have been avoided." (Konrad Adenauer)
  "History: An account mostly false, of events mostly unimportant, which are brought about by rulers mostly knaves, and soldiers mostly fools." (Ambrose Bierce, The Devil's Dictionary)
  Source: http://www.quotegarden.com/history.html (contains numerous other quotes on history and historians)
- **Kopiervorlage 9** (Seite 87) bietet Übungen zur Festigung des Lernwortschatzes.

Essay excerpt/ Video clip

The world as India

pp. 40–41

HINTERGRUNDINFO

Susan Sontag *was one of America's most influential intellectuals. She was internationally renowned for her ardent commitment and the breadth of her critical intelligence as well as her passionate activism for the cause of human rights. Susan Sontag was born in New York City in 1933 and grew up in Tucson, Arizona. She did graduate work in philosophy, literature, and theology at Harvard University and Saint Anne's College, Oxford. Sontag, whose books have been translated into 32 languages, published four novels, a collection of short stories and several plays as well as works of nonfiction. She wrote and directed four feature-length films and also directed plays in the United States and Europe. Her stories and essays were published in newspapers, magazines, and literary publications all over the world, including the New York Times, the New Yorker, the New York Review of Books and the Times Literary Supplement. In 2003 Susan Sontag was awarded the Peace Prize of the German Book Trade. Sontag, who firmly believed in the capacity of art to entertain, to inform and to transform, died in New York City in December 2004 of leukemia.*

Lernwortschatz *diversity, population, ethnic group, disparity, official language, vernacular, composition, precisely, native, conqueror, colonial, alien, foreign, to unify, diverse, to reinforce, pre-eminence, isolated, impoverished, unique, to advance, dominance, recent, to be involved in, to attain, to flourish, enterprise, economy, to employ, reservation, to dial, toll-free (AE), to compete, to erase, trace, to fail, salary, to outsource, to perform a task, error, virtually, college degree, booth, to be equipped with, to summon, cheerful, instructor, to acquire, idiom, elementary, to falter, to pass for sth, to be assigned, identity, occupation, religious denomination, marital status, reply, client, directions, operator, to let on, to pretend, routinely, to monitor, supervisor*

Materialien → **Online-Link: 601006-0016**

Brainteaser

1 *Thinking about India's ethnic and religious diversity and also the …*

Diese Aufgabe dient als Grundlage für eine vorbereitende Diskussion, bevor der Text von Susan Sontag gelesen wird.

Lösungsvorschlag ***Problems concerning administration and government***

- *Both the government and the administration must pay particular attention to treating all citizens fairly and equally, which might sometimes be very difficult.*
- *Government officials or administrators might find it hard or even impossible to meet the expectations and needs of the diversified citizenship.*
- *With more than 400 individual languages and 22 official languages, communication in general must often be very difficult.*
- *People whose mother tongue is not one of the officially accepted languages might have problems understanding important documents issued by the government or the administration.*
- *Speakers of languages which don't have official status might begin to struggle for its recognition and thus there might always be arguments and fights on the issue of languages.*
- *Real fluency in two or three languages is very difficult to achieve and thus the great number of languages in India is probably a general impediment.*

Possible solutions

- *Equality and fair treatment of all groups in society must be an integral part of the constitution and political and administrative practice.*
- *Government officials as well as administrators need to be thoroughly trained and need to be open-minded and tolerant towards citizens from a different ethnic or religious background.*
- *The English language might help the administration and the government to ensure mutual understanding.*
- *Official documents must be translated into 22 different languages, though this takes a lot of effort and might result in misunderstandings or even wrong translations.*

Brainteaser

2 *Explain the development and role of English as a lingua franca in India ...*

Vor der Textlektüre erfolgt noch ein Hinweis auf die *VIP file* zu Susan Sontag. Aufgabe 2 wird unmittelbar nach der Textlektüre als Überprüfung des Globalverständnisses bearbeitet.

Lösungsvorschlag *According to the text, there are sixteen "official languages" in India in addition to many more local languages which are only spoken in a particular region. Due to this diversity and because of the fact that 180 million Muslims inhabit India it is not very likely that the principal language, Hindi, will become the national language (ll. 1–5). Thus a language that is to be accepted by all the people living in India has inevitably to be a foreign language: "Just because it is alien, foreign, it can become the unifying language of a permanently diverse people" (l. 8). As it is not the native language of anyone nobody has an advantage over the others, and this means equal opportunities for everyone. The computer has enhanced the all-pervasiveness of the English language. At the same time "languages spoken by very small, isolated, impoverished peoples" (l. 13) have vanished. The reason for the fact that English is spoken in every part of the world is that it is spread by the media and that business people as well as scientists need a common language to communicate (ll. 16–18).*

Erweiterung L stellt folgende Aufgabe, die im Plenum besprochen wird: *Summarise the information the text gives about recent developments in the Indian economy and their causes and discuss possible global effects.* Die Ergebnisse werden stichpunktartig an der Tafel gesammelt. L macht die S zusätzlich noch auf den Cartoon aufmerksam. Die inhaltliche Aussage kann in die Zusammenfassung einbezogen werden.

Mögliche Lösung: *A new kind of enterprise has become vital to the software industry, which is so important to India's economy with its multi-billion dollar turnover: call centres. These call centres are maintained by corporations like IBM, Delta Airlines or chains of hotels and restaurants which have outsourced their customer service and tech support to India. A skilled workforce is being trained by these companies and thus enabled not only to give professional answers to the customers' questions, but also to talk with an American accent. The competition for these jobs is fierce and those who have finally made it get a very good salary compared to ordinary office jobs in India (l. 29). The companies still save on labour costs as the Indian employees are cheaper and presumably "perform the tasks better, with fewer errors, which is not surprising, since virtually all of them have college degrees" (ll. 32 ff.).*

Discussion of possible global effects of these developments

- *India seems on the way to becoming a first world economy with full employment, which will have fundamental consequences on the global economy.*
- *More and more companies are shifting their customer service and tech support to India, thus multinational companies are becoming dependent on India, as they train the workforce there and consequently can no longer rely on skilled employees in these branches in their own countries.*
- *On the other hand India's economy might become dependent on multinational firms.*
- *The consequence of this development is that the worldwide economy is becoming interconnected in a more complex way; thus globalisation is now clearly visible, not only in the production field but also in the service sector.*

Analysis

3 Comment on what Sontag reports about call centres …

Aufgabe 3 eignet sich als schriftliche **Hausaufgabe**. Hinweis auf die Wortmaterialien in der *Word bank* zu *International business*.

Lösungsvorschlag

I found it rather odd to read about how far multinational companies are going to make their customers believe they are talking to a fellow citizen rather than an employee answering their questions from his or her cubicle in India. I can understand that companies are forced to stay competitive and thus do everything to save on labour costs; however, in my view it is not really necessary to even provide fake biographies for the employees who are forced to lie to the customer and pretend to be a completely different person. In general I could not imagine assuming a different identity to do a job. However, I would be willing to pretend to be another person if the customer knew that I was acting a role; thus I could imagine taking over the role of an actor at a living history museum, like Plimoth Plantation, for example. But I would definitely not be prepared to lie to customers and be assigned a different name and a new biography.

Comprehension

4 [5] Look at the following tasks before you watch the video, …

Materialien → **Film 5 (India with Mark Tully: Present-day challenges)**

[5] Die S lesen zunächst die Fragestellungen aufmerksam durch, bevor der Videoclip zweimal gezeigt wird. Bei der Vorführung machen sie sich Notizen, auf deren Grundlage sie im Anschluss die Fragen in Partnerarbeit oder Kleingruppen bearbeiten. Eine Besprechung im Plenum schließt die Aufgabe ab.

Lösungsvorschlag

1. ***Visual contrast at the beginning of the clip***

- *The video clip starts with scenes showing congested, crowded streets; masses of people, seemingly not very wealthy, are on the move; some people are on motorcycles or bicycles, some are pulling or pushing carts loaded with various goods; others are carrying huge loads on their shoulders; there are small vans as well as tricycles, too, at the side of the streets.*
- *In stark contrast to this, the second scene shows a western-style mall. Window displays reveal global brands like Nike or Reebok. People dressed in western style wearing jeans, and pullovers, for example, are strolling along, eating fast food and are window-shopping.*

The shopping mall is/is not as I would have expected it

Individuelle S-Antworten.

2. ***Problems in the context of the reform and development of India's economy***

- *According to many economists, western consumerism cannot be the answer to India's special needs.*
- *In a multi-ethnic, pluralistic and diversified society which is trying to cope with three challenges at the same time, democracy, social transformation and economic transformation one cannot follow any set patterns.*
- *Thus reforms which are indigenous to Indians, which are of their own making, have to be undertaken.*

3. ***Perspective of international business leaders***
- *Whereas in the past India was a no-go area for foreign investors, now funds from abroad pour into Mumbai's stock exchange.*
- *However, according to international business leaders, India will attract less foreign investment than China in the future unless India's economic policies suit their needs.*

Implications of this perspective for India
- *The Indian government and administration must provide conditions which are favourable to the demands of international business and funds and thus meet their special needs.*
- *This would perhaps mean that local businesses would be less competitive than the huge international corporations and global funds and thus might eventually be merged with the more powerful western companies.*

4. ***Summary of the presenter's final thoughts on the situation***
- *Mark Tully thinks that India is now at a decisive crossroads. The question is how it will deal with its problems of persistent poverty and religious tensions.*
- *The presenter believes that India should not allow international business to dictate to the country in which direction the economy should be developed and reformed.*
- *Instead Indians should decide for themselves how to proceed in the future by taking into consideration the very special needs of the country.*
- *Mark Tully is convinced that India's economy must grow and expresses his hopes that India's unique culture which has provided so much space for so many religions as well as languages will survive.*
- *He hopes that India will be able to show to the world that unity in diversity can exist.*

Comment on these thoughts

Mark Tully argues very reasonably that India's economic policies should not be determined by international businesses but should be based on sustaining India's culture and diversity. I think this is a convincing statement. However, I assume it will be hard for India's government to reform India's economy in such a way that India's most pressing problems will be solved, its cultural identity will be saved and foreign investors will be satisfied.

Evaluation

5 [ååå] *After viewing: Do a role play in the form of a discussion …*

Die Klasse wird in Vierergruppen eingeteilt. Die S notieren sich zunächst Standpunkte und Argumente zu ihrer Rolle und üben die Diskussion ein. Im Plenum präsentieren einzelne Gruppen ihr Streitgespräch.

Lösungsvorschlag Individuelle S-Beiträge.

Novella excerpt

[5◎] The Gateway of India

pp. 42–43

HINTERGRUNDINFO

Paul Theroux *was born on April 10, 1941 in Medford, Massachusetts to a French-Canadian father and an Italian mother. Having graduated with a Bachelor of Arts degree, Theroux trained for the Peace Corps and then worked as a lecturer in Italy, Malawi, Africa and Singapore. He has written articles for various newspapers and magazines, such as "Playboy" or "The Christian Science Monitor". Theroux is the author of various acclaimed novels, short stories as well as travelogues. He is well known for his lively descriptions of life in foreign countries. Theroux currently divides his time between Cape Cod and Hawaii.*

The ***Gateway of India*** *faces out to Mumbai Harbour and is the first landmark which visitors coming to the city by boat can see. It was also the place where the last British troops took their leave from India in 1948. The arch is made of basalt and reinforced concrete and is 26 metres (85 ft) high. Construction began in 1911 to commemorate the royal visit of King George V. It was not completed until 1924. Today the gateway is a popular gathering spot for locals and tourists alike. It is also the place to be for balloon sellers, ice cream vendors, photographers, beggars as well as touts.*

Lernwortschatz *stifling, to drag on, boardroom, to reflect, archway, vendor, hawker, beggar, to gleam, industrialist, boldness, to wince, remark, to calculate, assortment, roof tile, sample, to manufacture, pad, dish, spicy, to stare at sb, edible, lethal, ordeal, reckless, deliberate, recently, to get divorced, to receive, engagement ring, as though, to spite sb, secular, to dread sth, to exceed, hideous, grief, to cease, to praise, to gloat over sth, discovery, sense, to assault, disgusted, appalled, anguish, physical, failure, futility, disease, misery, measure, supply, can, appropriate, confusion, to assign, outsourcing, to be desperate to do sth, bride, groom, disillusionment, to compound, to suffer, grateful, to prove to be sth*

Materialien → **CD, Track 5 • Online-Link: 601006-0017**

[5 ◉] Anhand der Fotos auf der Doppelseite diskutieren die S zunächst, welche Eindrücke ein Reisender aus einem westlichen Land von Indien bekommen könnte und welche Schwierigkeiten sich für einen Ausländer in der Begegnung mit der fremden Kultur ergeben könnten. Der Text wird vor der Bearbeitung der einzelnen Aufgaben einmal von der CD vorgespielt und anschließend noch einmal in Stillarbeit gelesen. Hinweis auf die *VIP file* zu Paul Theroux.

Analysis

1 *Characterise Dwight Huntsinger and explain what business ...*

Hinweis auf die Wendungen in der *Word bank*. Die beiden Teilaufgaben **a)** und **b)** werden am besten schriftlich bearbeitet. Insbesondere **b)** eignet sich als **Hausaufgabe**.

Lösungsvorschlag

a) *Dwight Huntsinger is an American lawyer who is currently on his second business trip to India. His task is to find outsourcing deals for his company, which he obviously does very successfully as "the firm was grateful, for India proved to be outsourcing heaven" (ll. 76 ff.). In the meetings with the Indians in the boardroom on the top floor of Jeejeebhoy Towers, which is within sight of the Gateway of India, he is seated at the head of the table, indicating that he chairs the meeting. Dwight Huntsinger seems to be a rather outspoken, straightforward man who is presumably not willing to give up very easily and who seems to be quite ambitious and strong-willed. His exchange with the industrialist M.V. Desai shows that he is tough in the negotiations and he knows very well how to treat the other party (ll. 13–17). Although he is absolutely disgusted at what he experiences in India, as the country "had exceeded even his fearful expectations" (l. 37) he returns to India, this time well-equipped to survive "his seven days of captivity in Mumbai" (l. 55). On the one hand this behavior shows that Huntsinger is able to cope with all the vagaries and that he seems to be able to make the best of a difficult situation. On the other hand, however, his way of dealing with the unknown things the country offers illustrates that he feels superior to this culture and that he is quite intolerant towards things he does not know. He reveals his loathing and revulsion towards India in a very honest, but rather rude way when he talks to Shah, the point man (ll. 47 ff.).*
Huntsinger is characterised as a very calculating person, who avoids showing emotions, so he doesn't seem to be able to cope with India's sensuality. India and the Indians are too physical, emotional, sensual for him. He seems to regard his trips to India as a kind of penance for his failed marriage: "India had been an ordeal for him, but he had chosen it in a willful way, knowing it was reckless (ll. 28 ff.). Thus the misery he felt in India only deepened his disillusionment with marriage (ll. 75 ff.).

b) *Huntsinger obviously despises and loathes India. When he decided to go to India he had expected the worst, but his expectations were exceeded as India turned out to be "dirtier, smellier, more chaotic and unforgiving than anywhere he'd ever been" (ll. 37–38). His experiences in India left him "mute and small" (l. 40) and "in this world of anguish he felt physically hurt by what he saw" (ll. 48–49).*
In contrast to the quotations on India on pages 4–5, Huntsinger only realises bleak and abhorrent aspects of the continent. Whereas Keith Bellows, for example, is overwhelmed by the richness of the country, its lushness of colours, its intensity of sounds, smells and tastes, Huntsinger cannot cope with this abundance of sounds and smells and visual impressions.
The author employs various stylistic devices to illustrate Huntsinger's views. First of all, the Gateway of India as a symbol of arrival in India serves to represent Huntsinger's success and the fact that he has managed to cope with all the obstacles and unpleasant things he associates

with India (ll. 4–5), but on the other hand Huntsinger does not really manage to get through to India because he refuses to get involved. Moreover, the Gateway is used to illustrate his unwillingness to find out more about the Indian culture and way of life (ll. 63 ff.).
Food serves a similar purpose. Huntsinger refuses to touch any Indian food and considers the dishes that are being served as poisonous (ll. 20 ff.). For his second trip to India he has brought an array of cans of food and soft drinks which he consumes in the bathroom of his first-class hotel room (ll. 53 ff). He does feel ashamed of his behaviour, however, but he considers this a necessary prerequisite. India, after all, is "not a place to enjoy but one to endure, like going down a dark hole to find jewels" (ll. 70 ff.).
On his first day of negotiating with his Indian business partners, Huntsinger comments on the food with the words "It's all nuts and cheese balls at this table" (l. 23). This statement can either be taken literally, referring to the dishes on the table. However, the words can also have another meaning, hinting at the mental state of the participants of the meeting (nuts) and also containing a sexual innuendo (balls). Nuts and balls can also plainly mean "nonsense". Thus, here the author uses a pun, a play on words.

Evaluation

2 *Examine and explain the way Shah and Huntsinger deal …*

Die beiden Teilaufgaben können in einer Partnerarbeitsphase erledigt werden. Die Ergebnisse werden anschließend im Plenum besprochen.

Lösungsvorschlag

a) *Shah, the point man who is Huntsinger's guide in everything, seems to be very proud of his country and its places of interest. He repeatedly suggests to Huntsinger places they could visit (ll. 60–62). However, Huntsinger regularly offends Shah, e.g. when he very plainly states that he is disgusted, frightened and appalled by what he sees and experiences (ll. 47 ff.).*
Huntsinger also insults Shah by refusing his suggestions and tells him that he wishes to see the Gateway of India, only to explain that he relishes it because he does not have to leave his hotel or the boardroom of the office building in order to see it. Shah apparently takes pride in the culture of his home country and wishes to show the foreigner as many places of interest as possible. He is very friendly and open and tries to be sociable, to get in touch with the American, whereas Huntsinger remains at a distance and does not want to get involved. He cannot cope with the different smells, sights, food and way of life which is characteristic of India. He feels repelled and is particularly appalled at the fact that "the Indians never ceased to praise it, gloating over it, saying how much they loved it" (ll. 41 ff.).

b) Shah: *You must try this excellent fish curry. This restaurant specialises in this traditional Indian dish – prawns, mussels, mackerel and a variety of exquisite spices. It's really, really good!*
Huntsinger: *I don't think so. It looks absolutely disgusting. Obviously the cook has put all the rubbish that he has found in his kitchen into this dish. And it smells awful!*
Shah: *I am very sorry that this does not appeal to you. What would you like to have for dinner then?*
Huntsinger: *How about a huge sirloin steak with a good barbecue sauce on top of it, served with some nice roast potatoes?*
Shah: *But … you can have that at home any time.*
Huntsinger: *That's exactly the reason why I would like to have it, because I'm missing it!*

Research

3 [💻] *Find out about the Taj Mahal in Agra and the …*

Zu Hause recherchieren die S weitere Infos zu den angesprochenen Sehenswürdigkeiten und präsentieren ihre Ergebnisse dann im Plenum.

Lösungsvorschlag

*The **Taj Mahal** is India's most famous landmark and is described as the world's most extraordinary monument ever built for love. Situated in Agra, India, this mausoleum was built by Mughal Emperor Shah Jahan in memory of his favorite wife, Mumtaz Mahal, who died giving birth to their 14th child in 1631. Grief-stricken, the emperor arranged for the construction of the Taj to begin in the same year. The Taj Mahal, which was not completed until 1653, is considered* *the finest example of Mughal architecture, a style that combines elements from Persian, Indian, and Islamic architectural styles. The spectacular mausoleum was designated a UNESCO World Heritage Site in 1983.*

*The **Elephanta Caves** are a complex of Shiva temple caves on Elephanta Island, an hour-long ferry ride from Mumbai. Elephanta Island was designated a UNESCO World Heritage Site in 1987. The origins and the identity of the artists of the temple caves, which are believed to date from about the 7th century, remain obscure. The caves house enormous statues, e.g. a 6.3 m (18 ft.) Mahesamurti statue depicting Shiva in his three-headed aspect: as Creator, Protector and Destroyer. Other sculptures praise Shiva's accomplishments, e.g. showing Shiva bringing the Ganges River down to Earth. However, many of the sculptures were damaged or destroyed by the Portuguese, who apparently used the Hindu gods as target practice in the 17th century. The Portuguese also gave the island its modern name, Elephanta, after they had found a large stone elephant near their landing place. The island with its exquisite caves is a worthwhile destination for tourists who want to escape from the hustle of Mumbai's streets and are interested in Hinduism.*

Newspaper articles

Fashion's dirty secret/Träume in Pink, Gold, Orange pp. 44–45

Lernwortschatz *to be credited with, to sweep, to increase, to swamp, embroidery, to eradicate, cramped, outskirts, suburbs, remote, to stitch, glistening, pattern, to ban sb from sth*

Materialien → **Online-Link: 601006-0018**

Brainteaser

1 Before reading: Think about the clothes you are wearing right now.

Im Plenum stellen die S zunächst ihre Kenntnisse und Vermutungen vor. Nach diesem L-S-Gespräch erfolgt die gemeinsame Textlektüre.

Lösungsvorschlag Individuelle S-Beiträge.

Comprehension

2 Describe in what sense child labour in India is a 'secret'. Point out …

Die Fragesellung wird im Plenum besprochen.

Lösungsvorschlag *Child labour in India is hidden from the public as it mainly takes place in small sweatshops in the slums of Delhi. Exporters of clothes, for example, say that there is no child labour in their factories. However, if the demand for particular items or services like embroidery cannot be met by the workers in their factories, the exporters need to subcontract some of the work and can no longer guarantee that child labour does not play a role in the manufacturing process. One supplier of western fashion companies argues that "It's not possible for everybody to check everything" (ll. 12 ff.). Thus approximately 100,000 children work for very little money up to 14 hours a day for the fashion industry "in hundreds of cramped, dusty workshops on the outskirts of Delhi" (l. 18).*

Analysis

3 Discuss: Child labour is preferable to starvation …

Die S notieren sich zunächst Punkte, die sie in der Diskussion vorbringen möchten. Die Diskussion kann in Form eines Kugellagers geführt werden: Diejenigen S, die die These eher befürworten, sitzen in einem inneren Kreis mit dem Gesicht nach außen gewandt, diejenigen S, die die These eher ablehnen, sitzen in einem äußeren Kreis gegenüber. Die sich jeweils unmittelbar gegenübersitzenden S tauschen in einem Zeitintervall von drei Minuten ihre Argumente aus, danach rutscht der äußere Kreis jeweils einen Platz weiter und es folgt erneut ein Austausch der Argumente.

Lösungsvorschlag ***Yes***

- *Unless the developing countries provide an adequate social security net and give parents a source of subsistence to prevent poor families from starving, child labour might be acceptable to avoid starvation, their own or that of their families.*
- *Child labour can indeed be seen as a necessary evil if the child's economic contribution is vital to the survival of the family. Although it deprives children of their childhood and bars them from getting an adequate education, it is still preferable to illness or death due to the family having an inadequate income.*
- *One might even argue that children working implies that they might get valuable work experience and the chance to learn a skill or trade at an early age. This might be considered equally as helpful as a formal school education, especially in less-developed countries in which job opportunities do not primarily depend on school education.*

No

- *Child labour bars children from enjoying a happy childhood, a time children should spend playing, learning and pursuing activities which develop their characters and bodies.*
- *Child labour deprives children from an adequate education; they will remain low-skilled workers for the rest of their lives.*
- *If one does not prevent child labour, the vicious circle of poverty, too little income and the need for children to help to support their families will never be broken.*

Evaluation

4 *Write a letter to* The Sunday Times *giving your reaction to the article …*

Wiederholung der Textsorte und Hinweis auf die *Word bank* zu *Letter to the editor.* Die Textproduktion erfolgt als schriftliche **Hausaufgabe**.

Lösungsvorschlag Individuelle S-Lösungen.

Evaluation

5 *Mediation: Bollywood has helped to popularise Indian style …*

Lösungsvorschlag *Bollywood cinema is a major economic factor in India. All in all, about 200 films are produced in Mumbai's dream factories every year. Approximately a further 600 films are produced in vernacular languages throughout the subcontinent. Bollywood superstars are worshipped just like gods and goddesses by their hard-working audience who mostly lead quite miserable lives. Bollywood productions, however, provide them with a three-hour-distraction from their tough lives in the 16-million-city of Mumbai with a fantasy world of glittering costumes and handsome heroes and heroines as well as song and dance. The films perfectly blend the different genres of romance and comedy, gangster movie and street ballad, video clip and meditation and thus resemble massala – the typical Indian blend of hot spices. The choreography is of particular importance for each movie. In fact, the dance numbers are "massala in massala" as they link up the different elements of the movie and at the same time consist of various ingredients themselves – they are a mixture of steps and gestures borrowing elements from classical Indian dance, regional folk dance, hip hop and jazz dance, Michael-Jackson-style and Ginger-Rogers-romance as well as ring-a-ring o'roses and free style.*

Novel excerpt

[6◎] Jasmine pp. 46–47

HINTERGRUNDINFO

Bharati Mukherjee *is an award-winning Indian-born American writer. She was born in 1940 in Calcutta to the wealthy owner of a pharmaceutical company. At the age of eight, she moved to England together with her family where they stayed for three years before returning to Calcutta. Bharati Mukherjee studied English gaining a BA and two MAs. She then attended a two-year creative writing course in the USA. In 1963, while studying at the University of Iowa, she met and married a Canadian student from Harvard, Clark Blaise. She earned her Ph.D. in English and Comparative Literature in 1969. She and her husband lived in Montreal and Toronto in Canada for more than a decade (1968–1980) before they returned to the United States. Mukherjee published her first novel "The Tiger's Daughter", in 1972. "Jasmine", her third novel, a much acclaimed piece of fiction, was published in 1989 and presents the attempts of a young Indian woman in the United States to adapt to the American way of life. Bharati Mukherjee is currently a professor in the department of English at the University of California, Berkeley.*

Lernwortschatz *mutual, penetrate, humidity, to crackle, crooked, gap, matchstick, to relate to, to be on good terms, to giggle, to prompt sb to do sth, satisfactory, expenses, to approve , to be repulsed, assumption, to blush, currently, unwed, awful*

Materialien → **CD, Track 6 • Online-Link: 601006-0019**

Brainteaser

1 *What do you think it is like for young people brought up …?*

Die S tauschen ihre Vermutungen im Plenum aus und begründen ihre Ansichten.

Lösungsvorschlag

Young people brought up in traditional Indian society might face several problems and difficulties when they emigrate to the US

- *They might feel alienated or overwhelmed by the different culture in the US.*
- *They might find it difficult to adapt to the American lifestyle or accept core American values and attitudes.*
- *They might feel misunderstood or not taken seriously by Americans who might not be able to acknowledge their different cultural and religious background.*
- *They might feel deprived of ways of showing and practising their religious faith.*
- *They might become homesick and long for their relatives, friends and acquaintances in their home village or city.*
- *They might find it difficult to retain their family ties because of the great distance between India and America.*
- *The young Indian immigrant might have different values and attitudes compared to the majority of Americans. Misunderstandings or even hostilities might arise due to cultural and religious differences.*

On the other hand, young Indian immigrants might also have various positive experiences

- *They might find job and career opportunities which would not have been attainable in their native country.*
- *They might be fascinated and deeply impressed by the different lifestyle in the US.*
- *They might be able to make friends easily as America is a pluralistic, multi-ethnic society.*
- *They might feel proud of their cultural background and happy to share and discuss their experiences and attitudes with their new American friends and acquaintances.*

Comprehension

2 *Listen, and talk about what is special about the Indian accent of the speaker.*

[6◎] Der Text wird einmal von der CD präsentiert. Die S verbalisieren ihre Eindrücke vom Akzent der Sprecherin. Im Anschluss erfolgt die individuelle Textlektüre. Hinweis auf die *VIP file* zu Bharati Mukherjee.

Lösungsvorschlag

- ***pronunciation of [r]:*** *the speaker puts particular stress on this sound especially in the middle or at the end of a word (like in "Taylor", l. 2, "river", l. 10, or "pair", l. 18) whereas in Received Pronunciation, [r] occurs only before a vowel; the [r] before a vowel is rolled by the speaker (e.g. in "American", l. 1, or "Broadway", l. 7)*
- *the speaker pronounces the* ***t and p sounds*** *in a rather crisp way (e.g. apartment, l. 1)*
- ***th-pronunciation:*** *in many words the speaker does not use the dental fricatives [θ] and [ð]) for the (th) but a dental plosive (d, t) instead (e.g. her pronunciation of "underneath", l. 6, "teeth", ll. 16 ff., or the definite article "the")*
- *the speaker does not clearly differentiate between* ***w and v sounds*** *(e.g. in "river", l. 10)*
- *the speaker does not differentiate between the* ***vowel sounds*** *[e] (as in "dress") and [æ] (as in "trap") (e.g. her pronunciation of "anyway", l. 45)*
- *both* ***word accent*** *and* ***sentence accent*** *differ from standard American or British English pronunciation; the speaker pauses in between words a native American or British speaker would usually link more closely (e.g. in "blondish _ _ _ beard", l. 18, or "pushed high _ _ _ in her hair", l. 19); she puts emphasis on syllables a native American or British speaker would leave unstressed (e.g. in "allergies", l. 34)*
- *all in all, she speaks rather slowly with a* ***syllabic rhythm***

Comprehension

3 *Point out why Jasmine is taken to meet the Hayes family.*

Die Fragestellungen werden gemeinsam im Plenum besprochen.

Lösungsvorschlag

a) *Jasmine is introduced to Taylor, Wylie and Duff Hayes by her friend Kate because she is going to live with the family and look after their little daughter Duff. After talking about this and that, Wylie offers Jasmine $95 a week to take care of their child and Jasmine happily accepts (ll. 38–41).*

b) *For Jasmine, the behaviour and attitudes of the Hayes family are odd and unfamiliar but at the same time fascinating and exciting. One of the first things she notices about them are their rather sloppy clothes and the fact that Taylor has teeth equally as crooked as hers (ll. 15 ff.). This is in stark contrast to what she would have expected professors to look like. Jasmine obviously shows great respect for academics and even suspects "the air itself to crackle with so much intelligence" (ll. 12 ff.) when they finally arrive at Claremont Avenue where all the apartments belong to Columbia professors. Jasmine is thrilled by the relaxed and laid-back way the Hayeses treat her. Although she feels inferior to them, they treat her like an equal person and do not behave in a condescending way at all, even though she doesn't really comprehend what they say (ll. 55–56). She considers "a professor who served biscuits to a servant, smiled at her, and admitted her to the broad democracy of his joking, even when she didn't understand it" (ll. 49–51) as "entirely American" (l. 51). The professor's attitude and way of life seem so extraordinary to her that she wants to fully comprehend his actions by watching and becoming a part of his life (l. 53).*
Jasmine is amazed at how naturally Duff, the Hayes's little girl, participates in the adults' conversations and how easily she could "relate to adults, call them by their first names" (ll. 23–24). The fact that she is being offered money "for sleeping with a child" (l. 40) is something Jasmine would not have expected.
There are other details, however, which seem to distress Jasmine. For her the fact that Wylie openly talks about why they had to adopt a child ("Low sperm count", l. 58) is awkward so that she blushes (l. 59). Adopting a child is a concept she cannot really relate to: "Adoption was as foreign to me as the idea of widow remarriage" (ll. 74–75).
She is equally embarrassed at the sight of "Barnard women … changing T-shirts … [who] wore nothing under their shirts and sweaters" (ll. 78–80). She feels repulsed by the fact that "even on the first morning [she] saw naked bodies combing their hair in front of dresser mirrors" (ll. 80–81), a fact which she attributes to the lack of shame in the American society.

c) *The sentence "I became an American in an apartment on Claremont Avenue …" (ll. 1–2) implies that living with the Hayes family has influenced and shaped Jasmine in such a fundamental way that she has given up her Indian identity and turned into an American, adopting a typically American lifestyle and attitude.*

Analysis

4 *Analyse the narrative techniques used by the author and the effect …*

Diese Aufgabe eignet sich als schriftliche **Hausaufgabe**.

Lösungsvorschlag

The story is told by a first-person narrator. The "I" is the central character, a young Indian who is about to live with an American family, who relates her first meeting with the Hayeses. The narrator recalls this day as some vital and extraordinary experience and illustrates this by describing details and commenting on particular things in a specific way. In various passages of the text the narrator describes the scenes from the point of view of an observer, e.g. in ll. 5–13 or ll. 14–22. These descriptions, however, also contain personal comments of the narrator in which she reveals her thoughts and expectations, e.g. "I expected the air itself to crackle with so much intelligence" (ll. 12 ff.), or "the first crooked teeth I'd seen in America" (l. 16) and "I had never seen a small child …" (ll. 22 ff.). By this narrative technique the reader becomes aware of the difference between the behaviour and attitudes of an ordinary American family and the assumptions and mental state of the Indian woman. The text is composed of a rather simple sentence structure. Many of the sentences consist of just a main clause; some contain simple subordinate clauses like relative clauses or participle and gerund constructions (e.g. ll. 1–4 or ll. 76–82). The vocabulary, too, is rather plain and simple. The style thus reflects the language skills that the narrator seemed to have at that point in her life ("I didn't have the slightest understanding of anything they said …" (l. 55).

Novel excerpt

[7 ◎] The Mistress of Spices pp. 48–49

HINTERGRUNDINFO

***Chitra Banerjee Divakaruni** is an acclaimed Indian-American author who was born in Calcutta, India, in 1956. She emigrated to the US in 1976 where she continued her education in the field of English by receiving a Master's degree from Wright State University in Dayton, Ohio, and a Ph.D. from the University of California, Berkeley. Together with her husband and two sons Divakaruni lives in Houston, where she currently teaches creative writing at the University of Houston. Divakaruni's works are largely set in India and the United States, and often focus on the experiences of South Asian immigrants, particularly on women who are torn between western and Indian cultures and values. Divakaruni is the author of the award-winning short story collection "Arranged Marriage" (1995).*

***"The Mistress of Spices"** is her first novel. It focuses on Tilo, the owner of a spice shop in Oakland, California, who is not the elderly Indian woman she appears to be. Tilo is a trained mistress of spices who supports her customers, predominantly first- or second-generation immigrants by evoking the magical powers of the spices of her homeland. The mistress of spices is trapped in an old woman's body and prohibited from leaving the shop. However, she yearns to join the world of mortals which enrages the spices. Thus Tilo must face the dire consequences of her disobedience. "The Mistress of Spices" was turned into an acclaimed film in 2005.*

Lernwortschatz *spice, potent, blister, bleached, to drip, bland, core, apprenticeship, reckoning, enticing, sting, remedy, enchanted, to tempt sb, sealed, jar, to flicker, cleanser, bumpy, to dangle, cloth, gravel, tear, to gather, eager, to crush, fragrant, scatter*

Materialien → **CD, Track 7 • Online-Link: 601006-0020**

[7 ◎] Der Romanauszug wird zunächst von der CD vorgespielt und das Globalverständnis geprüft. Die S lesen den Text anschließend noch einmal in Stillarbeit und bearbeiten Aufgabe 1. Hinweis auf die *Fact file* zu *The Ramayana*.

Brainteaser

1 The Mistress of Spices *(1997) is a novel about Tilo, …*

Lösungsvorschlag

- ***lanka, the dry chilli:** the most beautiful as well as potent of spices; child of the god of fire, Agni; the dry chilli brings taste to the bland earth; but lanka is also dangerous and must only* *be used as a last remedy; it frees from the evil; but it must only be used by the experienced (not before the "third level of apprenticeship", l. 9) (ll. 2–26)*

- ***cardamom:** opens people's eyes (ll. 69–70)*
- ***clove:** spice of compassion (l. 71)*
- *both **cardamom and clove** make people's breath smell sweet (l. 68)*
- ***cinnamon:** looks like a hollow dark bone but is also warm-brown like the skin (ll. 74–76); a friend-maker but also destroyer of enemies: it will help Jagjit to find friends who cheer him up and support him; the cinnamon will also give Jagjit enough strength to stop others from bullying him (ll. 75–81)*

Comprehension

2 *Describe how the text portrays the experience of Indian immigrants …*

Diese Aufgabe eignet sich als Partnerarbeit. Hinweis auf die *VIP file* zu Chitra Banerjee Divakaruni.

Lösungsvorschlag

a) *The first-person narrator is an Indian immigrant who makes her living selling spices. She recalls her encounter with the 10-year-old Jagjit and his mother, both Indians who have been living in America for only a short while. The little boy can't speak English yet (ll. 31 ff., ll. 61 ff.). He is being bullied at school because he knows only Punjabi and wears a "green turban that the kids at school make fun of" (l. 39). The two first English words he has learned are "idiot" and "asshole" as he is being called these names by the other children at school and in the playground. His mother is a resolute woman who does not seem to realise the terrible things her son has to put up with. She chides him when he comes home in his dirty and torn clothes and forces him to go to school although he is obviously very much afraid of this (ll. 62 ff.). She reminds him that she is not "made of money" (ll. 51–52) and that his "father is killing himself working working at the factory" (ll. 62 ff.).*

The first-person narrator seems to be the only person to understand Jagjit. She smiles at him and gives him some sweets. She intends to support him with the help of her spices: "Cardamom which I will scatter tonight on the wind for you" (l. 69) which will open the eyes of Jagjit's teacher and mother or "cinnamon, hollow dark bone that I tuck unseen in your turban just before you go" (ll. 74–75) which will help Jagjit to find a friend and give him strength to defend himself against the abusive behavior of the other children.

The text reflects the dreams, hopes and desires but also the pain and struggle of Indian immigrants in America in the tale of the owner of the spice shop. Jagjit and his mother experience different aspects of the new life: Whereas his mother seems to continue in the USA the traditional role of an Indian woman who is responsible for the home, more or less staying apart from the influences of the foreign lifestyle, shopping for Indian food in an Indian store, Jagjit has to go to school and confront the other kids everyday, fully experiencing that he is an outsider. She sees the good opportunities for her family and does not understand what it is like to face the unkind and harsh sides of the new world because she can avoid confronting them.

b) *The spices seem to be a chance for the Indian immigrants to connect to their old life, the one they led before emigrating to the US. The shared knowledge about cooking traditional food and the mythical role of the spices create a sense of belonging and a way for the Indians to remain linked to their original culture. When they enter the shop, they enter a world that lies apart from the harsh reality and competition outside. The shop and the spices represent a kind of shelter, a world of magic where everything is possible, where there is always hope, a cure for every illness. The narrator sees herself in a position to fight against the injustice of the world outside by using the magical power of the spices. It can be doubted though if this kind of attitude is helpful to people settling in another country because it is aimed at remaining separate, creating a kind of parallel culture rather than at integration. However, the main dilemma of immigrants is trying to get on in the society they have come to live in without losing their own cultural identity.*

Analysis

3 *Comment on how the style of writing reflects the content of the text.*

Diese Aufgabe eignet sich als schriftliche **Hausaufgabe**.

Lösungsvorschlag *The text is written by a first-person narrator, the Indian immigrant Tilo, owner of a spice shop in Oakland, California. In the text, past and present events are presented as they come into the narrator's mind by random association. The narrator also addresses the reader directly, e.g. in the very first line of this extract: "Let me tell you about chillies." (l. 1). In other parts, the narrator talks to the spices as if they were people she is having a conversation with: „Lanka, lanka. Sometimes I roll your name over my tongue." (l. 14). These passages reflect the otherness and exoticism of the spices and give the text an immediacy and vividness that arouse the reader's interest. The descriptions of the spices are very sensual: "The chilli sings" (l. 4), it is "blister-red" (l. 2), bringing " taste" (l. 6), an "enticing sting" (ll. 14–15). The text excerpt introduces the relationship between the spices and their mistress: It is a relationship of love (l. 7) and respect (ll. 9–10, l. 16). On the one hand they provide her with enormous power, but on the other she has to be careful and treat them with respect because they can be very dangerous. That danger is emphasised again and again: "Its other name is danger" (l. 3), the chilli is compared to a bird of prey, "a hawk" (l. 4), associated with "fire" (l. 5), a "sleeping volcano" (l. 8/9), "the day of reckoning" (l. 11), "suicide and murder" (ll. 12–13).*

Indian words are frequent in the text where food and spices are described. Thus the importance of food for Indian identity is emphasised. The sentences are mainly short, sometimes words are repeated, and it is full of imagery, such as in the description of the spices (see above) or "the sack of our existence" (l. 12), "tall as wild bamboo" (ll. 28–29), "the colour of a parrot's breast" (ll. 44–45). The tense is the present tense, which makes the reader experience the sensuality of the text and the emotions that are conveyed very directly. All these elements create a magical, mystical style reminiscent of oral storytelling, which is probably supposed to be associated with Indian culture.

The contrast between Jagjit's and his mother's perception of life in the USA is also reflected in the language that is used: His mother uses incomplete sentences, they do not sound like idiomatic English, sometimes incorrect: "Jaggi what you meaning ...?" (l. 62). She generally overuses the progressive form. She uses repetitions for emphasis, which is probably due to the influence of her mother tongue: "waiting waiting" (ll. 42–43), "working working" (l. 63). All this indicates that she is still very much at home in her Indian way of life. Jagjit's experiences with his fellow students are extremely negative, which is expressed by the use of English swear words: "idiot" (l. 34) repeated three times for emphasis and "asshole" (l. 47). The effect is enhanced by the fact that Jagjit's name means "world-conqueror" (l. 40). All in all, the author uses language effectively to contrast the two different cultures.

Analysis

4 *Compare and contrast* Jasmine *and* The Mistress of Spices.

Zusatzmaterial → **Klausurvorschlag 4 • Revision file 4**

Diese Aufgabe wird am besten im Plenum besprochen.

Lösungsvorschlag

Atmosphere created in the excerpt of "Jasmine"
- *liveliness*
- *happiness*
- *positive expectations*

Main focus
- *hopes and expectations of a young Hindu woman on the brink of her new and exciting life in America*
- *the Indian protagonist is fascinated by the American way of life, although she is also a bit unsettled about some aspects of the American lifestyle*
- *however, she has a predominantly positive outlook and admires most of those aspects of American attitude and life that she is confronted with (l. 53: "I wanted to ... be a part of it.")*

Atmosphere created in the excerpt of "The Mistress of Spices"
- *darkness*
- *exoticism*
- *menace*

Main focus

- *the difficulties of a young Indian boy facing discrimination and trying to come to terms in his new environment shortly after emigrating to the US*
- *the Indian protagonists are struggling to cope with the new situation and do not really seem to identify with their new home*
- *their traditional way of life and their old values seem to be of a great importance to them and they try to defend their culture in a hostile environment*

Erweiterung

- Wenn die Zeit vorhanden ist, empfiehlt es sich, den Film in Ausschnitten oder ganz anzusehen, um zu zeigen, wie sich die Haltung der Protagonistin Tilo entwickelt. Dadurch, dass sie sich in einen Amerikaner mit hispanischem Hintergrund verliebt, ist sie irgendwann gezwungen, den Schutz ihres Ladens zu verlassen und sich zu entscheiden, in welcher Welt sie leben will bzw. wie sie es schaffen kann, ihre Wurzeln zu behalten und trotzdem in der neuen Welt eine Heimat zu finden.
- Zum Abschluss des *Topics* füllen die S noch *Revision file* 4 (Themenheft, Seite 63) aus. Ein Lösungsvorschlag befindet sich hier im Lehrerheft auf Seite 112.

Sequenzplaner – Differenzierungshinweise GK / LK

Topic 1 A plural country Seite 4–13

Titel	SB-Seite / Unterrichts-stunden	Textsorte	Thema	Kernsequenz (GK + LK)/ Vertiefung (LK)
Some quotes about India	SB, S. 4/5 1–2 Stunden	*Combination of visuals, quotes, map*	*First information on India*	Kernsequenz 1 (GK + LK)
Indian identity is forged in diversity	SB, S. 6/7 2 Stunden	*Newspaper article*	*Indian national identity*	Vertiefung 1 (LK)
A visit to the Cow Product Research Centre	SB, S. 8/9 2 Stunden	*Book extract*	*The role of the sacred cow in Hinduism*	Kernsequenz 2 (GK + LK)
Hindu gods	SB, S. 10 1 Stunde	*Factual information*	*Hinduism*	Kernsequenz 3 (GK + LK)
What Happened to the Elephant?	SB, S. 11 1–2 Stunden	*Poem*	*Hindu Gods Ganesha and Shiva*	Vertiefung 3 (LK)
A visual dialect	SB, S. 12/13 2 Stunden	*Novel excerpt*	*Living between the castes*	Kernsequenz 4 (GK + LK)

Topic 2 The wounds of history Seite 14–25

Titel	SB-Seite / Unterrichts-stunden	Textsorte	Thema	Kernsequenz (GK + LK)/ Vertiefung (LK)
Timeline/Mark Tully's India	SB, S. 14 1-2 Stunden	*Timeline, interviews*	*British rule in India*	Kernsequenz 1 (GK + LK)
Why can't we be friends?	SB, S. 15 1 Stunde	*Novel excerpt*	*India during the British Raji*	Vertiefung 1 (LK)
Father to a nation, stranger to his son	SB, S. 16/17 2 Stunden	*Newspaper article*	*Mahatma Gandhi and his eldest son*	Kernsequenz 2 (GK + LK)
Cracking India	SB, S. 18 1–2 Stunden	*Novel excerpt*	*The Partition of India*	Kernsequenz 3 (GK + LK)
Indian independence	SB, S. 19 1 Stunde	*Factual information*	*The two independent states of India and Pakistan*	Vertiefung 3 (LK)
Exit Wounds – The legacy of Indian Partition	SB, S. 20/21 2 Stunden	*Newspaper commentary*	*The legacy of Partition*	Kernsequenz 4 (GK + LK)
Muslims – India's new 'untouchables'	SB, S. 22/23 2 Stunden	*Newspaper article*	*Muslims in India*	Vertiefung 4 (LK)
Looking across the border	SB, S. 24/25 1–2 Stunden	*Book excerpt*	*The India-Pakistani border*	Kernsequenz 5 (GK + LK)
Indische Presse bezichtigt Pakistans Geheimdienst der Terrorhilfe	SB, S. 25 1 Stunde	*German Internet news article*	*The relationship between India and Pakistan*	Vertiefung 5 (LK)

Topic 3 Different worlds Seite 26–35

Titel	SB-Seite / Unterrichts-stunden	Textsorte	Thema	Kernsequenz (GK + LK)/ Vertiefung (LK)
Quotations by Gandhi and Ambedkar	SB, S. 26/27 1–2 Stunden	*Combination of visuals, quotes, statistics, interview*	*Rural India vs. city life*	Kernsequenz 1 (GK + LK)
'Long live Suttee', cried the mob	SB, S. 28/29 2 Stunden	*Newspaper article, video clip*	*Widows in Hinduism/ The Barefoot College*	Kernsequenz 2 (GK + LK)
Hunger	SB, S. 30/31 2 Stunden	*Novel excerpt*	*Life of poor peasants in India*	Vertiefung 2 (LK)
The Solitude of Emperors	SB, S. 32/33 2 Stunden	*Novel excerpt*	*Living between the castes*	Kernsequenz 3 (GK + LK)
A shocking transformation	SB, S. 34/35 1–2 Stunden	*Interview transcript, video clip*	*Changes in India*	Vertiefung 3 (LK)

Topic 4 East meets West Seite 36–49

Titel	SB-Seite / Unterrichts-stunden	Textsorte	Thema	Kernsequenz (GK + LK)/ Vertiefung (LK)
India's magic works wonders!	SB, S. 36/37 1–2 Stunden	*Combination of visuals, cartoon, Internet article*	*The fascination of India*	Kernsequenz 1 (GK + LK)
A family of Anglophiles	SB, S. 38/39 2 Stunden	*Novel excerpt*	*Anglophiles in India*	Vertiefung 1 (LK)
The world as India	SB, S. 40/41 2 Stunden	*Essay excerpt, cartoon, video clip*	*Information technology in India*	Kernsequenz 2 (GK + LK)
The Gateway of India	SB, S. 42/43 2 Stunden	*Novella excerpt*	*A business trip to India*	Vertiefung 2 (LK)
Fashion's dirty secret	SB, S. 44/45 1 Stunde	*Newspaper article*	*Child labour in India*	Kernsequenz 3 (GK + LK)
Träume in Pink, Gold, Orange	SB, S. 45 1 Stunde	*German newspaper article*	*Bollywood*	Vertiefung 3 (LK)
Jasmine	SB, S. 46/47 2 Stunden	*Novel excerpt*	*Immigrant experiences*	Kernsequenz 4 (GK + LK)
The Mistress of Spices	SB, S. 48/49 1–2 Stunden	*Novel excerpt*	*Immigrant experiences*	Vertiefung 4 (LK)

KV 1: Quiz on India

p. 4, ex. 1

How well do you know this country? Mark the correct answer for each question.

1. What is the capital of India?

☐ a) Lahore ☐ b) Mumbai
☐ c) New Delhi ☐ d) Kolkata

2. Many of the cities in India have been renamed. One example is Mumbai. What was Mumbai called before it was renamed?

☐ a) Nurmahal ☐ b) Madras
☐ c) Bombay ☐ d) Murwara

3. Which country does not share a common border with India?

☐ a) Pakistan ☐ b) Bangladesh
☐ c) Bhutan ☐ d) Laos

4. What is the national animal of India?

☐ a) Indian Elephant ☐ b) Royal Bengal Tiger
☐ c) Lion ☐ d) Cougar

5. Which year marked the independence of India from British rule?

☐ a) 1951 ☐ b) 1948
☐ c) 1918 ☐ d) 1947

6. What was the name of the freedom fighter of India whose doctrine of non-violent resistance has become famous?

☐ a) Arundhati Roy ☐ b) Mahatma Gandhi
☐ c) Mohammed Jinnah ☐ d) Jawaharlal Nehru

7. Which is the longest river in India?

☐ a) The Ganges ☐ b) The Brahmaputra
☐ c) The Indus ☐ d) The Yangtze

8. What is the main language of India?

☐ a) Hindi ☐ b) Punjabi
☐ c) Bengali ☐ d) Sanskrit

9. Which term does not refer to one of the castes in India?

☐ a) Brahmins ☐ b) Kshatriyas
☐ c) Vaishyas ☐ d) Mohandas

10. Which is the second largest religious group in India?

☐ a) Hindus ☐ b) Muslims
☐ c) Buddhists ☐ d) Sikhs

11. Who became the first female Prime Minister of India?

☐ a) Benazir Bhutto ☐ b) Yulia Tymoshenko
☐ c) Indira Gandhi ☐ d) Pratibha Patil

Abi Workshop Englisch
India Lehrerheft
ISBN 978-3-12-601016-0

KV 2: Map of India

p. 4, ex. 1

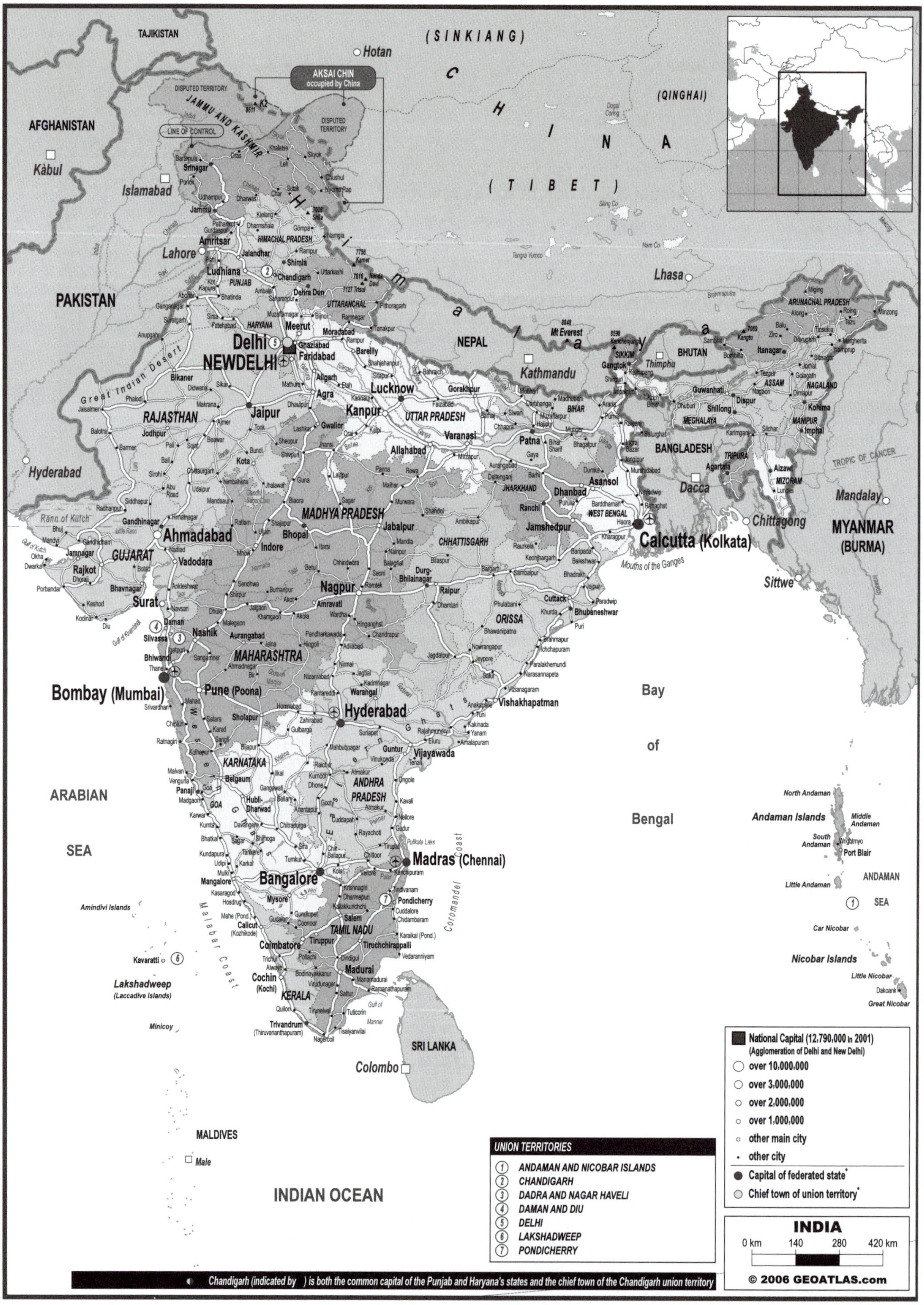

Abi Workshop Englisch
India Lehrerheft
ISBN 978-3-12-601016-0

KV 3: Working with words

p. 7, ex. 4

a) *Match the adjectives to their definitions or synonyms.*

g.	1. secular	a. surprising/amazing/astonishing
	2. eligible	b. unthinkable
	3. archetypal	c. having all the important qualities that make sb/sth a typical example of a particular kind of person or thing
	4. startling	d. with a recognisable difference
	5. ancient	e. obvious
	6. inconceivable	f. able to have or do sth because of having the right qualifications
	7. sumptuous	g. relating to worldly things
	8. distinguishable	h. precious, very expensive and looking very impressive
	9. apparent	i. very old; having existed for a very long time

b) *Find verbs that express the opposite of the verbs and definitions.*

1. being able to do without	↔	
2. to detest/hate sb	↔	
3. not sticking firmly to sth	↔	
4. to disappear	↔	
5. not providing enough of what sb/sth needs in order to live or exist	↔	
6. to give up	↔	

c) *Use the following nouns in an English sentence.*

1. notion: ______________________________
2. compatriot: ______________________________
3. partition: ______________________________
4. creed: ______________________________
5. conviction: ______________________________
6. complexion: ______________________________

d) *Add a verb to finish the following phrase and sentence.*

1. to ____________________ higher taxes
2. The streets were ____________________ with tourists.
3. It took him a while to ______________________________ to the idea.

Abi Workshop Englisch
India Lehrerheft
ISBN 978-3-12-601016-0

KV 4: What do you remember about India's past?

p. 14

Put in the missing information and thus complete the timeline.

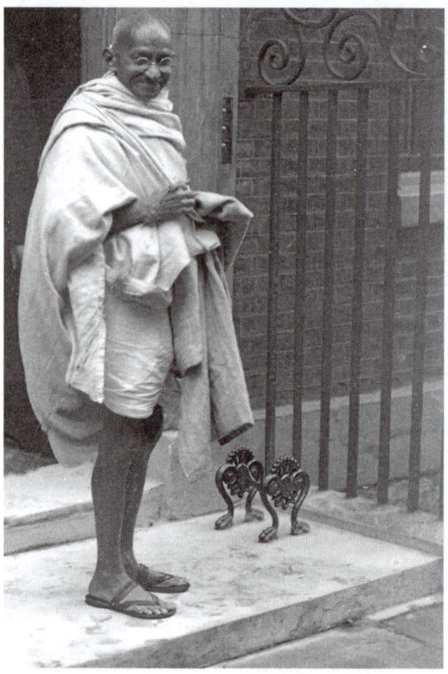

16th/17th century	European ____________________ starts in India
1600	British ____________________ founded
1757	Beginning of ____________________, restricted in 1784
19th century	India is opened up to ____________________ and ____________________
1857	____________________ against land taxation and interference with inheritance laws
1858	Beginning of the ____________________, i.e. the British Crown takes over rule in India
1876	Queen Victoria becomes ____________________
late 19th century and early 20th century	First steps towards Indian ____________________
1914–1918, World War I	India provides ____________________ and ____________________ for the war
1940	____________________ idea of a separate Muslim territory supported
1942	____________________ starts his "Quit India" movement
1947	British ____________________; India's independence; ____________________ into two separate states: India and ____________________

Klett

Abi Workshop Englisch
India Lehrerheft
ISBN 978-3-12-601016-0

KV 5a: Some important literary terms – Part I Genre, plot, theme, structure

p. 15, ex. 2

[ ] *Read the definitions and hints regarding **genre, plot, theme and structure**. Then examine these aspects of the text (E.M. Forster, "Why can't we be friends?", students' book, p. 15) in detail and use your results to illustrate how Forster portrays the situation in India at the time and the relationship between the Indians and the British in general. Note the list of useful phrases.*

Literary genre

Poetry, drama and the novel constitute the three main kinds of literature. A novel is a fictitious narrative in prose, usually of considerable length and complexity, in which characters and connected sequences of events representative of real life are portrayed in a plot.

Plot

The plot is the interplay between the sequences of events and the characters – their statements, actions and thoughts.

Theme

The theme is the dominant idea in a literary text or the purpose of the author.

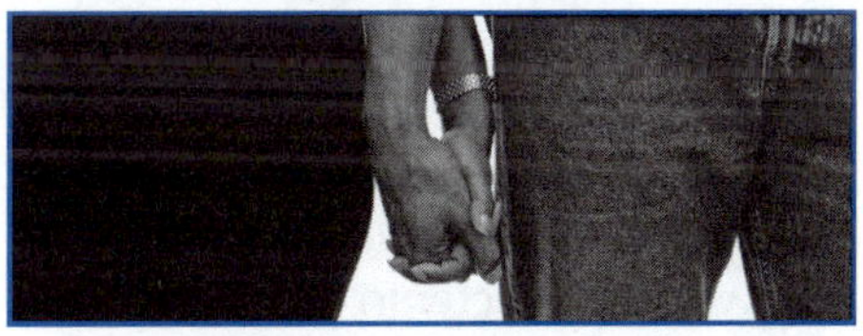

Structure

The way in which the parts of the narrative are connected together, arranged and organised.

Useful phrases

The plot/structure of the action	revolves around dramatises is based on focuses on	the conflict between the author's purpose/intention to the interaction between the argument between
This novel	is concerned with deals with evolves around	the theme of
The problem of …	constitutes provides is/forms	the main/dominant/central theme.
The author/writer	focuses on is predominantly concerned with is mainly interested in	the theme of
This extract	is concerned with deals with	

Abi Workshop Englisch
India Lehrerheft
ISBN 978-3-12-601016-0

KV 5 b: Some important literary terms – Part II Narrator and point of view

p. 15, ex. 2

[ ] *Read the definitions and hints regarding **narrator and point of view**. Then examine these aspects of the text (E.M. Forster, "Why can't we be friends?", students' book, p. 15) in detail and use your results to illustrate how Forster portrays the situation in India at the time and the relationship between the Indians and the British in general. Note the list of useful phrases.*

*In a fictional text the author, the **narrator** and the characters are not identical. The narrator can be considered as the "storyteller" or a "second self", i.e. an implied author. The **narrator's view** then governs the story-telling process and determines the perspective through which the reader perceives the events of the narration. Basically there are three types of narrators. However, the types can be mixed and the **point of view** can be changed in the course of the story.*

first-person narrator ("I"), limited point of view	third-person limited narrator	third-person omniscient narrator
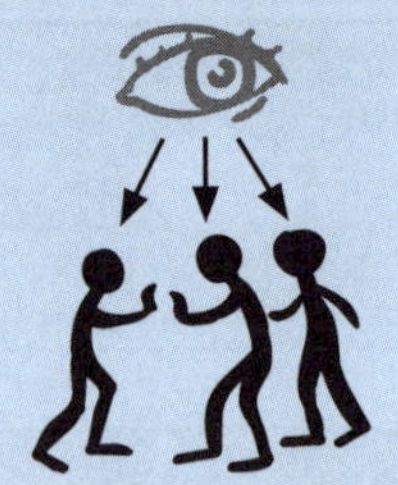	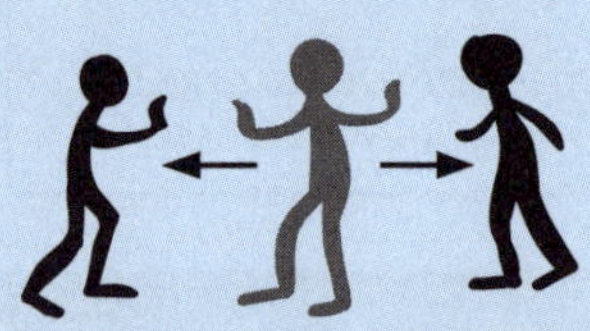	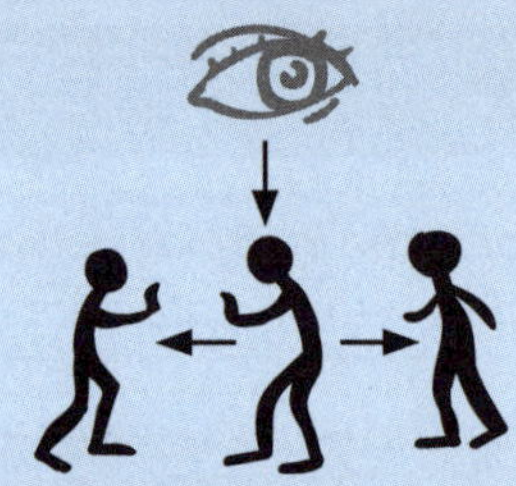
■ story is told from the inside	■ story is told from the outside	■ story is told from the outside
■ narrator is either identical with a character in the story or is an observer/witness of the action	■ narrator describes the events though the "filter" of one character's mind and thus only knows about the feelings and opinions of a particular character	■ this type of narrator knows everything about the characters, their feelings and thoughts and the events in the story
■ you get to know only what the character knows, thus the point of view is limited	■ the narrator is not identical with this character, however	■ sometimes the omniscient narrator even comments on the characters' behaviour, the story or the writing itself
	■ another possibility: story is told by several third-person narrators with shifting points of view	

Useful phrases		
The author	makes use of employs	a third-person point of view. a shifting point of view.
The passage	is presented	from an omniscient/limited point of view.
The events	are portrayed	from the point of view of a single character/several characters/the protagonist/...
The narrator	is	omniscient. limited in his knowledge. himself a character in the narrative.
X	is stands	the viewpoint character. outside the story.

Abi Workshop Englisch
India Lehrerheft
ISBN 978-3-12-601016-0

KV 5c: Some important literary terms – Part III Characters

p. 15, ex. 2

[ ] *Read the definitions and hints regarding **characters**. Then examine these aspects of the text (E. M. Forster, "Why can't we be friends?", students' book, p. 15) in detail and use your results to illustrate how Forster portrays the situation in India at the time and the relationship between the Indians and the British in general. Note the list of useful phrases.*

***Character** can be revealed in basically two ways – by direct characterisation and by indirect characterisation:*
- ***Direct characterisation** is based on direct statements: When the narrator or another character in the story mentions a character trait directly (e.g. "X is a reliable and trustworthy").*
- ***Indirect characterisation** is based on evidence derived from what a character says and does and how he feels. The readers have to interpret what a character is like from what goes on in the narrative itself.*

*Additional clues may be provided by other **characters** in the narrative, e.g. when they talk about the character and his past or comment on his actions and behaviour, his appearance, etc.*

Useful phrases
This character is described/presented/portrayed/depicted/characterised as
The basic traits of X's character are
One of X's striking characteristic traits is
X is characterised by one predominant character trait
X appears to be a … character.
X forms a/stands in contrast to Y.

Abi Workshop Englisch
India Lehrerheft
ISBN 978-3-12-601016-0

KV 5 d: Some important literary terms – Part IV Imagery and symbolism

p. 15, ex. 2

*Read the definitions and hints regarding **imagery and symbolism**. Then examine these aspects of the text (E.M. Forster, "Why can't we be friends?", students' book, p. 15) in detail and use your results to illustrate how Forster portrays the situation in India at the time and the relationship between the Indians and the British in general. Note the list of useful phrases.*

Imagery

***Imagery** denotes the use of language which represents objects, actions, feelings, thoughts and ideas through the use of comparisons or associations. Most often authors use similes and metaphors to establish a connection between one object or idea and another, thus making certain phenomena clearer to the reader.*

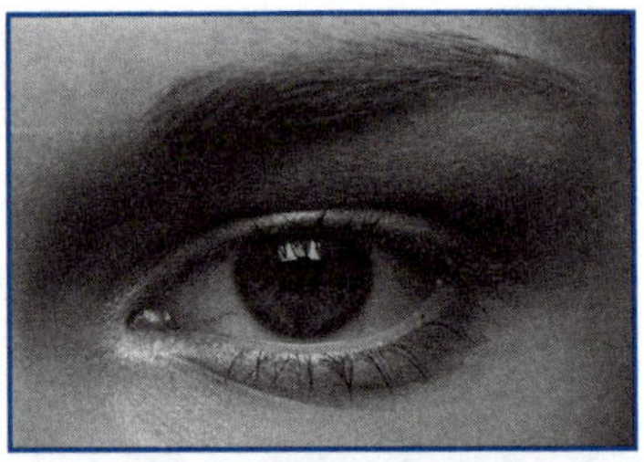

Simile

*A **simile** is an explicit comparison between two things which are basically quite different using words such as "like" or "as":*
She walks like an angel./I wandered lonely as a cloud. (Wordsworth)

Metaphor

*A **metaphor** is a comparison between two things which are basically quite different without using like or as. While a simile only says that one thing is like another, a metaphor says that one thing is another, although this cannot be literally true. Thus metaphors indicate resemblance without expressing it directly. (adj = metaphorical)*
All the world's a stage./And all the men and women merely players. (Shakespeare)

Symbol

*A **symbol** is something concrete, e.g. a person, an object, an image, a word or an event that stands for or is associated with a more general quality or situation, something abstract or invisible (e.g. white is a symbol of purity in Western cultures.)*

Useful phrases

The author	employs/relies on makes use of/uses compares X and Y establishes an analogy between A and B	a metaphor in line a simile in line
The simile/metaphor in line …	suggests/implies illustrates	
The phrase	calls forth associations of	
A	stands for/symbolises is a symbol of/serves as a symbol of signifies/represents	B

Abi Workshop Englisch
India Lehrerheft
ISBN 978-3-12-601016-0

KV 6: Mother Teresa

p. 17, ex. 1

a) *Put in the correct verb forms: active or passive, simple or progressive forms. Choose the correct tenses. Be careful: Some of them are non-finite forms, gerunds or participles.*

Mother Teresa ______________________ (to be) a famous woman of Indian citizenship who ______________ (to leave) her mark on history and who ____________________ (to consider) a living saint, particularly by the poor and abandoned that she ____________________ (to devote) her life to. Born Agnes Bojaxhiu on August 26, 1910, in Skopje, then part of the Ottoman Empire and later Macedonia, she ____________________ (to take) the name Sister Teresa in Ireland, where she ____________________ (to join) the Sisters of Loreto, an Irish community of nuns with missions in India. After a few months she ____________________ (to send) to India. From 1931 to 1948 Mother Teresa ____________________ (to teach) at St. Mary's High School in Calcutta, but the suffering and poverty she __________________ (to observe) outside the convent walls __________________ (to make) such a deep impression on her that in 1948 she __________________ (to receive) permission from her superiors __________________ (to leave) the convent school and _____________ (to devote) herself to __________________ (to work) among the poorest of the poor in the slums of Calcutta. In 1950, with permission from the Vatican, Mother Teresa ____________________ (to start) her own order, "The Missionaries of Charity", which today ____________________ (to comprise) branches in many countries, __________ (to provide) effective help to the poor. The order also ____________________ (to undertake) relief work in the wake of natural catastrophes such as floods, epidemics, and famine, and for refugees. In addition, the order __________ (to have) houses where alcoholics, homeless people, and AIDS sufferers __________ (to take) care of. Mother Teresa's work ______________ (to recognise) throughout the world and she ____________________ (to receive) a number of awards and distinctions. In 1979 she __________ (to award) the Nobel Peace Prize for her humanitarian work. At her request, the traditional banquet ______________ (to cancel) so the $7,000 in costs ______________________ (can • to go) to the poor. "We need to tell the poor that they are somebody to us," she told the audience of rich and honoured guests, "that they too ______________________ (to create) by the same loving hand of God, to love and be loved." Mother Teresa ______________________ (to beatify) on October 19, 2003, by Pope John Paul II, ______________________ (to reach) the ranks of the blessed in the shortest time in the history of the church. Mother Teresa ______________________ (to die) on September 5, 1997. Her biographer and friend Navin Chana ______________________ (to say) she ____________________ (to remember) as someone who "gave the word compassion a new dimension".

b) *Conditional clauses: Put in the right verb forms.*

1. If Mother Teresa's order stopped operating its missions, hundreds of hospices and houses for the poor and disadvantaged ____ (must • to close).
2. If Mother Teresa ______________________ (not • to be) disturbed by the poverty surrounding her in Calcutta, she might have continued teaching.
3. If Mother Teresa hadn't dedicated her life to the sick and hungry, she ___________________________ ___________________________ (not • to award) the 1979 Nobel Peace Prize.

Abi Workshop Englisch
India Lehrerheft
ISBN 978-3-12-601016-0

KV 7: An imaginary interview

p. 29, ex. 6

[👥] *Work in pairs. One of you takes the role of a reporter writing about the suttee of the widow Kuttu Bai, the other one of*

- *one of Kuttu's sons, or:*
- *a villager attending the suttee, or:*
- *a police officer involved in the investigation*

After conducting the first interview, change roles and act out another interview with another person from the list above.

Reporter

Useful vocabulary

When did you first …?

How did you feel/react when …?

Did you attempt to …?

Do you think Kuttu Bai …?

What happened when …?

✂ -

Interview partner

Kuttu's son

villager

Useful vocabulary

Well, let me begin with …

There's evidence for/proof that …

I admit/regret/insist …

It's vital to keep in mind that …

It's certainly difficult to imagine that …

You may wonder why …

police officer

Abi Workshop Englisch
India Lehrerheft
ISBN 978-3-12-601016-0

KV 8 a: Analysing cartoons – Part I

p. 37, ex. 4

A cartoon is usually a combination of a drawing with a text. Cartoonists aim at criticising or poking fun at current events, developments and trends in politics, society, the economy, etc., institutions or individuals.

*Basically there are **three major steps** you should keep in mind when you analyse a cartoon:*

Before you start talking about the cartoon or writing down an analysis of it,

- ***note down** your first impressions and the associations that you have when you look at the cartoon,*
- ***consider** the source of the cartoon (e.g. which magazine or newspaper published it), the date of publication and the target group of the cartoon: knowing about the context (if provided) of the cartoon is important for the interpretation of it.*

Start your analysis of the cartoon with an introductory sentence referring to the context of the cartoon and a general statement on the message/the aim of the cartoonist.

Keep in mind the following aspects for your …

1. Description of the cartoon

- *Describe all the elements in the cartoon which relate to the message of the cartoon in detail; in order to describe activities displayed in the cartoon, use the present progressive.*
- *Pay particular attention to symbols the cartoonist uses in order to refer to sth else.*
- *Closely examine the text(s) – refer to the title, caption, speech/thought bubble(s), label(s) etc. and find out whether there is a contrast between picture and text; also record any important dates or numbers that appear in the cartoon.*

2. Interpretation of the cartoon

- *Explain what political/social/economic etc. event or idea the cartoon is referring to.*
- *Point out what key people or groups are part of the cartoon's message and describe how these are portrayed.*
- *Find out how the caption, title, label(s), or speech/thought bubble(s) in the cartoon contribute to the cartoon's message.*
- *Identify the irony, puns, symbols, exaggerations the cartoonist uses and their effect.*
- *Summarise the overall message and aim of the cartoonist.*

3. Evaluation of the cartoon

- *Say whether you think that the method chosen by the cartoonist effectively conveys the intended message.*
- *Try to point out which people/what special (interest) groups would agree/disagree with the cartoon's message and why.*

Of course, not all of these aspects might apply to a particular cartoon. But the hints above will help you to give a detailed description, an adequate interpretation and a reasonable evaluation of the cartoon.

Abi Workshop Englisch
India Lehrerheft
ISBN 978-3-12-601016-0

KV 8 b: Analysing cartoons – Part II

p. 37, ex. 4

Analyse the cartoon using the words and phrases in the Word bank.

Word bank

- The cartoon by … was first published in … ridicules/pokes fun at/mocks/aims at criticising …
- In the first panel/in the panel on the left/in the middle/centre of the cartoon/at the top/bottom/on the left/right/in the top left-hand/bottom right-hand corner/in the background/foreground/…
- … is drawn realistically/is distorted/exaggerated/…
- … is a symbol of/stands for/implies/refers to/alludes to/…
- … is a reference/an allusion to/a hint/…
- … shows/reveals/points to the fact that …
- The cartoon aims at criticising/ridiculing/poking fun at/is supposed to satirise/condemn/mock/make fun of/…
- The cartoon depicts …
- The cartoonist's point seems to be/is (not so) obvious/…
- Presumably the message/intention/aim of the cartoonist is …

Abi Workshop Englisch
India Lehrerheft
ISBN 978-3-12-601016-0

KV 9: Vocabulary work

p. 39, ex. 2

a) *Core vocabulary: Fill in the missing parts.*

1. to ____________________ or to ____________________ means to dislike and have no respect for sb/sth or to view with contempt
2. to be very excited and pleased: ____________________
3. to love sb/sth very much: ____________________
4. the feeling of liking or loving sb/sth very much and caring about them: ____________________
5. to destroy, to knock down a building: ____________________
6. to catch or take control of sb/sth: ____________________
7. feelings of respect and slight fear; feelings of being very impressed by sth/sb: ____________________

b) *Explain the following words in English.*

1. translucent: ____________________
2. dowry: ____________________
3. plump: ____________________
4. contemporary: ____________________

c) *Working with an English-English dictionary.*

1. *Look up the word "Anglophile" (p. 39, l. 12) in your dictionary and write down the definition. In how far does the entry differ from the definition of the "Reader's Digest Great Encyclopaedic Dictionary"?*

____

____

____

2. *Note down all the other compound nouns containing "Anglo" that your dictionary lists together with an explanation of the words.*

____

____

____

3. *In some passages, Chacko uses very high-flown language. Look at the following statement by Chacko where he explains to the children that history was like an old house at night (p. 39, ll. 44 ff.). Try to replace the marked words by more sophisticated words. You can make use of your dictionary for this task.*

"But we can't **go in** (____________________), **because** (____________________) we've been locked out. And when we **look in** (____________________) through the windows, all we **see** (____________________) are shadows. And when we **try** (____________________) to listen, all we hear is a whispering. And we cannot **understand** (____________________) the whispering, ..."

Abi Workshop Englisch
India Lehrerheft
ISBN 978-3-12-601016-0

Lösungen zu den Kopiervorlagen

Kopiervorlage 1
1. – c) New Delhi, 2. – c) Bombay, 3. – d) Laos, 4. – b) Royal Bengal Tiger, 5. – d) 1947, 6. – b) Mahatma Gandhi, 7. – a) The Ganges, 8. – a) Hindi, 9. – d) Mohandas, 10. – b) Muslims, 11. – c) Indira Gandhi

Kopiervorlage 3
a) 1. – g., 2. – f., 3. – c., 4. – a., 5. – i., 6. – b., 7. – h., 8. – d., 9. – e.
b) 1. to require, 2. to cherish sb/sth, 3. to adhere to sth, 4. to emerge, 5. to sustain, 6. to endure
c) 1. I only have a vague notion of your job. What do you actually do?
2. Frank and Sue both come from Ireland, so they are compatriots.
3. The partition of Germany lasted from 1949 until 1990.
4. In India you can find people of many creeds – Hindus, Muslims and Christians.
5. It is my personal conviction that the death penalty should be abolished.
6. She has got a dark complexion. Is she from southern Europe?
d) 1. impose, 2. thronged, 3. accustom himself

Kopiervorlage 4
16th/17th c. – European **trading** starts in India
1600 – British **East India Trading Company** founded
1757 – Beginning of **Company rule**, restricted in 1784
19th c. – India is opened up to **private investment** and **missionaries**
1857 – **Indian Rebellion** against land taxation and interference with inheritance laws
1858 – Beginning of the **British Raj**, i.e. the British Crown takes over rule in India
1876 – Queen Victoria becomes **Empress of India**
late 19th c. and early 20th c. – First steps towards Indian **self government**
1914–1918, World War I – India provides **money** and **troops** for the war
1940 – **Lahore/Pakistan Resolution**: idea of a separate Muslim territory supported
1942 – **Mahatma Gandhi** starts his "Quit India" movement
1947 – British **withdrawal**; India's independence; **partition** into two separate states: India and **Pakistan**

Kopiervorlage 5
1. Genre, plot, theme, structure
- Novel; extract focuses on the exchange between the Muslim physician Dr. Aziz and the British headmaster Cyril Fielding at the time of the British Raj.
- The fictitious characters are representative of the two conflicting parties during the British rule in India, the Indians and the British; the verbal exchange of the two men might be typical of the conflict between the two sides.
- The plot focuses on the argument between Aziz and Fielding, thus depicting the two opposing attitudes regarding the British rule in India.
- This extract is concerned with the relationship between Indians and the British; the author wants to point out that although there are animosities and strong negative emotions, the individual people still like each other and want to be friends.
- The central theme, the ambiguous relationship between the Indians and the British, is highlighted by the structure of the text: whereas more than two thirds of the extract focus on the conflicting notions of the two men, lines 29–31 hint at their real feelings and suggest that they really want to be friends; however, the last part of the extract illustrates that the circumstances do not allow the formation of a stable friendship.

2. Narrator and point of view
- The author makes use of a third-person omniscient narrator who tells the story from the outside and knows about the feelings and thoughts of Fielding an Aziz.
- This omniscience becomes obvious when the narrator reveals the protagonists' emotions and inner monologues (e.g. ll. 15 ff.; ll. 20 ff.).
- The narrator even presents the attitudes of animals and inanimate objects: "But the horses didn't want it … the earth … the temples, the tank, the jail, the palace … they didn't want it …" (ll. 32–36).
- The narration is characterised by an impressive immediacy due to this narrative technique and creates a very vivid impression of the relationship between Indians and the British at that time.

Abi Workshop Englisch
India Lehrerheft
ISBN 978-3-12-601016-0

3. Characters

- The two protagonists are characterised as rather hot-headed and excited (ll. 1 ff.; ll. 10 ff.).
- Aziz is obviously not able to control himself: "… in an awful rage danced this way and that, not knowing what to do …" (ll. 23–24).
- Similarly to the Muslim doctor, Fielding is also described as being in a state of great agitation.
- Fielding is also characterised by his frequent use of irony and subtle hints revealing his contempt for Aziz's suggestions (ll. 20 ff.).
- Despite all the feelings of rage and their respective aggressiveness, however, both Aziz and Fielding are portrayed as affectionate towards each other (ll. 28–29; ll. 30–31).
- The characterisation of the protagonists depicts the ambiguity not only of the relationship between the two men but of the relationship of the Indians and the British in general, which seem to be characterised by feelings of hatred, contempt, frustration, etc. but at the same time by feelings of respect, affection and even friendship.

4. Imagery and symbolism

- The author employs a simile in lines 8–9: "the scenery, though it smiled, fell like a gravestone on any human hope"; the scenery, which also serves as a personification, stands for the difficult circumstances under which Fielding and Aziz live in the time of the British Raji and which do not enable them and in general the Indians and the British to live in friendship and harmony; thus people's hope for a better future will be destroyed.
- The last paragraph of this extract abounds in allusions to the difficulties that the two men and thus the Indians and the British in general will not be able to overcome in order to form a stable friendship: "But the horses didn't want it … the earth … the temples, the tank, the jail, the palace … they didn't want it …" (ll. 32–36).

Kopiervorlage 6

a) Mother Teresa was a famous woman of Indian citizenship who (has) left her mark on history and who is considered a living saint, particularly by the poor and abandoned that she devoted her life to. Born Agnes Bojaxhiu on August 26, 1910, in Skopje, then part of the Ottoman Empire and later Macedonia, she took the name Sister Teresa in Ireland, where she (had) joined the Sisters of Loreto, an Irish community of nuns with missions in India. After a few months she was sent to India. From 1931 to 1948 Mother Teresa taught at St. Mary's High School in Calcutta, but the suffering and poverty she observed outside the convent walls made such a deep impression on her that in 1948 she received permission from her superiors to leave the convent school and devote(d) herself to working among the poorest of the poor in the slums of Calcutta. In 1950, with permission of the Vatican, Mother Teresa started her own order, "The Missionaries of Charity", which today comprises branches in many countries, providing effective help to the poor. The order also undertakes relief work in the wake of natural catastrophes such as floods, epidemics, and famine, and for refugees. In addition, the order has houses where alcoholics, homeless people and AIDS sufferers are taken care of. Mother Teresa's work has been/was recognised throughout the world and she received a number of awards and distinctions. In 1979 she was awarded the Nobel Peace Prize for her humanitarian work. At her request, the traditional banquet was cancelled so the $7,000 in costs could go to the poor. "We need to tell the poor that they are somebody to us," she told the audience of rich and honoured guests, "that they too have been created by the same loving hand of God, to love and be loved." Mother Teresa was beatified on October 19, 2003, by Pope John Paul II, reaching the ranks of the blessed in the shortest time in the history of the church. Mother Teresa died on September 5, 1997. Her biographer and friend Navin Chana says/said she will/would be remembered as someone who "gave the word compassion a new dimension".

b) 1. If Mother Teresa's order stopped operating its missions, hundreds of hospices and houses for the poor and disadvantaged would have to be closed. 2. If Mother Teresa hadn't been disturbed by the poverty surrounding her in Calcutta, she might have continued teaching. 3. If Mother Teresa hadn't dedicated her life to the sick and hungry, she wouldn't have been awarded the 1979 Nobel Peace Prize.

Kopiervorlage 8

The cartoon refers to the fundamental changes that countries like China and India are currently undergoing, developing from poor countries characterised by the deprivation of their population, to serious powers in the global economy, with a population competing for jobs with the western workforce.
In the first panel you can see a mother with her little son at the dinner table. The boy is frowning at his plate, obviously not really willing to finish his meal. His mother says: "Finish your dinner – there are people in China and India who are starving". The title of this first panel is "yesterday", whereas it is "today" for the second panel. In this picture basically the same scene is depicted – a mother is sitting at a table with her son. The son seems to be a bit older and he is dealing with some schoolwork, with exactly the same look on his face as the boy in the first panel. Here the mother says: "Finish your homework – there are people in China and India who are starving for your job".

Abi Workshop Englisch
India Lehrerheft
ISBN 978-3-12-601016-0

The cartoon depicts the growing importance of India and China as economic powers in the world and the effects of this on the job market in other countries. Whereas previously both countries were so poor that children in the western world were reminded not to waste any food because of starvation in India and China, today parents are worrying about the job prospects of their children with people in India and China competing for jobs in the global market. By using the word "starving" in the two speech bubbles, the cartoonist contrasts the desperate situation of the people in these two countries in the past and the eagerness and striving for success of today's inhabitants of India and China. Thus he illustrates that the economic success of India and China will have considerable consequences for the young in western countries.
In my opinion the two panels effectively convey the cartoonist's intended message. It makes people aware of the fundamentally changing role of countries which were formerly considered as developing countries in today's globalised world.

Kopiervorlage 9

a) 1. to scorn or to disdain, 2. to be thrilled, 3. to adore sb/sth, 4. affection, 5. to demolish, 6. to capture, 7. awe

b) 1. light can pass through it, but it's not transparent, 2. in some cultures a wife or her family or a husband or his family must pay money and/or give property to their partner when they get married, 3. having a soft, round body; slightly fat, 4. belonging to the same time

c) 1. Anglophile (according to the *Oxford Advanced Learner's Dictionary*): a person who is not British but who likes Britain or British things very much; definition is less comprehensive and differentiated than the one given by the *Reader's Digest Great Encyclopaedic Dictionary*

2. Anglo-American (no explanation given in the *Oxford Advanced Learner's Dictionary*):
- Anglo-Catholic: a member of the part of the Church of England that is most similar to the Roman Catholic Church in its beliefs and practices
- Anglomania: an extremely strong admiration for England or English customs
- Anglo-Norman: a form of Norman French spoken in England in the Middle Ages
- Anglophobia: hatred or fear of England or Britain
- Anglophone: a person who speaks English, especially in countries where English is not the only language that is spoken
- Anglo-Saxon: 1. a person whose ancestors were English; 2. an English person of the period before the Norman Conquest; 3. Old English

3. enter, since/as, peek, discern/spot, attempt, comprehend

Abi Workshop Englisch
India Lehrerheft
ISBN 978-3-12-601016-0

Klausurvorschlag Topic 1: The White Tiger (by Aravind Adiga)

"The White Tiger", which was published in 2008 and won the Man Booker Prize for the same year, is the debut novel by Indian author Aravind Adiga.

The narrator, Balram Halwi, tells the story in a series of letters to His Excellency Wen Jiabao, the prime minister of China, on the eve of his journey to India. Balram does not only write about his rise from lowly origins in a part of India he calls "the Darkness" to his current position as a successful entrepreneur in Bangalore's "Electronic City", but also reveals his views of Indian society and politics.

Like all good Bangalore stories, mine begins far away from Bangalore. You see, I am in the Light now, but I was born and raised in the Darkness.

But this is not a time of day I talk about, Mr. Premier! I am talking of a place in India, at least a third of the country, a fertile place, full of rice fields and wheat fields and ponds in the middle of those fields choked with lotuses and water lilies, and water buffaloes wading through the ponds and chewing on the lotuses and lilies. Those who live in this place call it the Darkness. Please understand, Your Excellency, that India is two countries in one: an India of Light, and an India of Darkness. The ocean brings light to my country. Every place on the map of India near the ocean is well off. But the river brings darkness to India – the black river.

Which black river am I talking of – which river of Death, whose banks are full of rich, darf, sticky mud whose grip traps everything that is planted in it, suffocating and choking and stunting it?

Why, I am talking of Mother Ganga, daughter of the Vedas, river of illumination, protector of us all, breaker of the chain of birth and rebirth. Everywhere this river flows, that area is the Darkness.

One fact about India is that you can take almost anything you hear about the country from the prime minister and turn it upside down and then you will have the truth about that thing. Now, you have heard the Ganga called the river of emancipation, and hundreds of American tourists come each year to take photographs of naked sadhus at Hardwar or Benaras, and our prime minister will no doubt describe it that way to you, and urge you to take a dip in it.

No! – Mr. Jiabao, I urge you not to dip in the Ganga, unless you want your mouth full of feces, straw, soggy parts of human bodies, buffalo carrion, and seven different kinds of industrial acids.

I know all about the Ganga, sir – when I was six or seven or eight years old (no one in my village knows his exact age), I went to the holiest spot on the banks of the Ganga – the city of Benaras. I remember going down the steps of a downhill road in the holy city of Benaras, at the rear of a funeral procession carrying my mother's body to the Ganga.

Kusum, my granny, was leading the procession. Sly old Kusum! She had this habit of rubbing her forearms hard when she felt happy, as if it were a piece of ginger she was grating to release grins from. Her teeth were all gone, but this only made her grin more cunning. She had grinned her way into control of the house; every son and daughter-in-law lived in fear of her.

My father and Kishan, my brother, stood behind her, to bear the front end of the cane bed which bore the corpse; my uncles, who are Munnu, Jayram, Divyram, and Umesh, stood behind, holding up the other end. My mother's body had been wrapped from head to toe in a saffron silk cloth, which was covered in rose petals and jasmine garlands. I don't think she had ever had such a fine thing to wear in her life. (Her death was so grand that I knew, all at once, that her life must have been miserable. My family was guilty about something.) My aunts – Rabri, Shalini, Malini, Luttu, Jaydevi, and Ruchi – kept turning around and clapping their hands for me to catch up to them. I remember swinging my hands and singing, "Shiva's name is the truth!"

We walked past temple after temple, praying to god after god, and then went in a single file between a red temple devoted to Hanuman and an open gymnasium where three body builders heaved rusted weights over their heads. I smelled the river before I saw it: a stench of decaying flesh rising from my right. I sang louder: "... the only truth!"

Then there was a gigantic noise: firewood being split. A wooden platform had been built by the edge of the ghat, just above the water; logs were piled up on the platform, and men with axes were smashing the logs. Chunks of wood were being built into funeral pyres on the steps of the ghat that went down into the water; four bodies were burning on the ghat steps when we got there. We waited our turn.

In the distance, an island of white sand glistened in the sunlight, and boats full of people were heading to that island. I wondered if my mother's soul had flown there, to that shining place in the river. I have mentioned that my mother's body was wrapped in a silk cloth. This cloth was now pulled over her face; and logs of wood, as many as we could pay for, were piled on top of the body. Then the priest set my mother on fire.

"She was a good, quiet girl the day she came to our home," Kusum said, as she put a hand on my face. "I was not the one who wanted any fighting."

I shook her hand off my face. I watched my mother. As the fire ate away the silk, a pale foot jerked out, like a living thing; the toes, which were melting in the heat, began to curl up, offering resistance to what was being done to them. Kusum shoved the foot into the fire, but it would not burn. My heart began to race. My mother wasn't going to let them destroy her.

Abi Workshop Englisch
India Lehrerheft
ISBN 978-3-12-601016-0

Underneath the platform with the piled-up fire logs, there was a giant oozing mound of black mud where the river washed into the shore. The mound was littered with ribbons of jasmine, rose petals, bits of satin, charred bones; a pale-skinned dog was crawling and sniffing through the petals and satin and charred bones. I looked at the ooze, and I looked at my mother's flexed foot.

This mud was holding her back: this big, swelling mound of black ooze. She was trying to fight the black mud; her toes were flexed and resisting; but the mud was sucking her in, sucking her in. It was so thick, and more of it was being created every moment as the river washed into the ghat. Soon she would become part of the black mound and the pale-skinned dog would start licking her.

And then I understood: this was the real god of Benaras – this black mud of the Ganga into which everything died, and decomposed, and was reborn from, and died into again. The same would happen to me when I died and they brought me here. Nothing would get liberated here.

I stopped breathing.

This was the first time in my life I fainted.

I haven't been back to see the Ganga since then: I'm leaving that river for the American tourists!

(1182 words)

Annotations

line 12: **Bangalore –** India's third most populous city and the capital of the Indian state of Karnataka
line 28: **darf –** foul
line 30: **to stunt –** to prevent from growing or developing
line 41: **sadhu –** a Hindu holy man, especially one who lives away from people and society
line 41: **Hardwar** (also spelled Haridwar), **Benaras –** cities situated on the river Ganges and considered as holy by Indians
line 45: **feces –** excrement
line 46: **carrion –** the decaying flesh of dead animals
line 85: **ghat –** steps leading down to a river or lake
line 85: **log –** a thick piece of wood used for construction or fuel

Tasks

1 Contents/Comprehension

a) What does the narrator mean by his statement "India is two countries in one" (ll. 22–23)?

b) Summarise what happens at the funeral of the narrator's mother and point out the significance of the event for the narrator.

2 Form/Analysis

a) Explain these phrases as they are used in the text:
"ponds … choked with lotuses and water lilies" (ll. 18–19);
"… and urge you to take a dip in it" (l. 43);
"a giant oozing mound of black mud" (l. 110).

b) Analyse the narrative perspective and the style and comment on their effect.

3 Comment/Text production

a) In lines 39–41 the narrator says that "… hundreds of American tourists come each year to take photographs of naked sadhus at Hardwar or Benaras, …".
How, in your opinion, should foreign tourists behave in order not to violate the feelings of the local population? Write a comment of about 150 words.

b) Could you personally imagine spending your holidays in India? Give reasons for your opinion.

Abi Workshop Englisch
India Lehrerheft
ISBN 978-3-12-601016-0

4 Mediation

Read the article below and summarise the most important aspects in German.

Out of the Darkness: Adiga's White Tiger rides to Booker victory against the odds

After an "emotionally draining" and closely fought final judging session, Aravind Adiga, one of the two debut novelists on the Man Booker shortlist, was last night awarded the £50,000 prize for The White Tiger, a bracingly modern novel about the dark side of the new India. […]

The White Tiger takes a sharp and unblinking look at the reality of India's economic miracle. Its antihero and narrator, Balram Halwai, is a cocksure, uneducated young man, the son of an impoverished rickshaw driver. By lying, betraying and using his sharp intelligence, Balram makes his ascent into the heady heights of Bangalore's big business.

The writing of the novel, said Adiga, had come out of his career as a journalist, and his encounters – as a relatively privileged middle-class man – with members of India's underclass.

"Class is a boring topic to write about. Big divides are not what people are interested in. But it's the most pressing concern – because other things spring out of it, like terrorism and instability," he said. "The book has done very well in India – and there is a need for books like this.

"Something extraordinary is happening between the rich and the poor. Once, there was at least a common culture between rich and poor, but that has been eroded, and people have noted that." […]

[Michael Portillo, the chair of the judges,] said that Adiga "undertakes an extraordinary task – he gains and holds the attention of the reader for a hero who is a thoroughgoing villain".

He also praised the work's attention to "important social issues: the division between rich and poor, and issues on a global scale. And it is extremely readable." The main criterion for the prize, he said, was: "Does this book knock my socks off? And this did."

[…]

(302 words)

ISBN 978-3-12-601016-0

Klausurvorschlag Topic 2: 'The Queen's Hinglish' gains in India

New Delhi — Ill-concealed smirking at the peculiarities of Indian English has long been a handy fallback for travel writers, who delight in transcribing misspelled menus, garbled hotel signs and awkward idioms. Naturally, this has always been viewed in India with irritation. […]

Bollywood scriptwriters have also milked the struggles of nonproficient English speakers for easy humor. But a recent side effect of India's growing economy and burgeoning national self confidence is the emergence of a new pride in Indian English, in all its forms.

Three recent books published here chart the growing, global reach of Hinglish – a blend of English and Hindi.

The title of Binoo K. John's new study of the language, "Entry From Backside Only" (a sign commonly seen in alleyways) misleadingly suggests this will be another exercise in ridicule. Instead it is a celebration.

"My idea was not to sneer at Indian English but to look at the way it is growing and becoming a language in its own right, like American English," John said. The book is a history of how English endured after Indian independence, tracing how Gandhi's decision to use it as a nation-building tool (having first rejected it as the language of slavery) was vital to its survival. It describes how the language has evolved, plucking sentence constructions and vocabulary from Hindi and the 30 other languages spoken here and mixing them with English.

"I believe this happy blend of Hindi and English will become a globally accepted form of English in 20 years or so," John said. "More and more people will use it without fear of being laughed at. We are not afraid of speaking in the way that we want to anymore. There is no longer any fear of grammatical puritans coming and telling us it should not be like that."

In "The Queen's Hinglish", another recent book on the theme, Baljinder K. Mahal writes that more people speak English in South Asia than in Britain and North America combined, with India alone accounting for more than 350 million English speakers.

"Although the practice was previously frowned upon by purists, people there are becoming more and more comfortable with mixing words from languages such as Hindi, Urdu, Punjabi with English," she writes. "This means that Hinglish, as this modern blend of standard English, Indian English and South Asian languages is popularly known, could soon become the most widely spoken form of English on earth."

She predicts that words like prepone (the opposite of postpone, to bring forward), or airdash (to travel by plane at short notice) or eve-teasing (for sexual harassment) could spread internationally.

"The purists – as they always do – have lost the battle," she writes. "Hinglish, once seen as the lingo of the uneducated masses, is now trendy – the language of the movers and shakers."

Vaishna Narang, a professor of linguistics at Delhi's JNU University, said the shift was noticeable.

"People used to attach a snob value to British English and received pronunciation. Today no one bothers about that. We are much more concerned about a functional English," she said.

She too attributed the change to the country's growing prosperity. "There is a much, much greater sense of confidence in ourselves and our language. People no longer look at Indian music and culture and language as in any way substandard or vernacular."

English newspapers are sprinkled more liberally with Hindi than they would have been a decade ago. Television advertising is now rarely in the clipped British English tone that once characterized it, said Nima Namkhu, senior creative director of Publicis in Delhi.

"Ten years ago, directors tried to get proper accents, to make sure the grammar was perfect," he said. "Now it's much more about how people on the street talk, a mix of Hindi and English. We are still moving away from memories of being a colony, towards being a nation of our own. This is part of that." […]

Andy Kirkpatrick, a professor at the Institute of Education in Hong Kong and author of "World Englishes", said that the rise of Indian English was inevitable.

"The world is about people for whom English is a learned language doing business with other people for whom English is a learned language," he said.

"Indian English is certainly likely to become more and more powerful."

(726 words)

Annotations

line 4: **garbled –** confused
line 10: **burgeoning –** beginning to grow or developing rapidly
line 69: **vernacular –** the language spoken in a particular area or by a particular group, especially one that is not the official or written language

Abi Workshop Englisch
India Lehrerheft
ISBN 978-3-12-601016-0

Tasks

1 Contents/Comprehension

a) Summarise what the authors of the three recently published books on Indian English found out about the role of this language in today's India in contrast to the past.

b) Explain why, according to the text, the role of Indian English has changed and how it will develop in the future.

2 Form/Analysis

a) Explain these clauses as they are used in the text:
"Ill-concealed smirking at the peculiarities of Indian English has long been a handy fallback …" (ll. 1–2);
"Hinglish, once seen as the lingo of the uneducated masses, is now trendy – the language of the movers and shakers." (ll. 56–58)

b) Explain the function of the headline.

3 Composition/Text production

Point out the role of the English language in our globalised world. Write a composition of about 150 words.

Abi Workshop Englisch
India Lehrerheft
ISBN 978-3-12-601016-0

Klausurvorschlag Topic 3: India's malnutrition dilemma

"This is a country on the make." The speaker was a young assistant to one of India's rising political stars. And from his perspective, it did look that way. We were sitting in the lobby restaurant of New Delhi's luxurious Taj Mahal Hotel. That evening, the Taj was not only the place for a government reception following Prime Minister Manmohan Singh's decisive re-election victory, but it was also the scene of a huge party for the aptly named Yes Bank as it celebrated $100 million in financing for a new private hospital.

India is indeed booming: receptions of this kind have become commonplace since the early 1990s. The pace of change is impressive by any standard, and even more so in a country that, as recently as the late 1980s, had an economy in which it was said you needed the intercession of a member of Parliament just to get a telephone line. Today, middle-class Indians can enjoy many of the same pleasures and habits as their opposite numbers in Shanghai or Berlin, from cappuccino bars to multiplexes. It is hard to spend time in any major Indian city without getting the sense that the middle class is optimistic about their country's prospects.

When Lloyd Blankfein, chairman of Goldman Sachs, declares that the 21st century will be India's and that of the other so-called BRIC countries (Brazil, Russia and China), he has sound reasons for saying so. The self-confidence of the Indian corporate elite is even more arresting. Mukesh Ambani, head of one of the country's principal conglomerates, expressed a common view when he insisted that the 21st century "belongs" to India – though he largely attributes this to demography, contrasting India's young population with the aging populations of the United States, Western Europe, Japan and China.

But there is a ghost at the party, and its name is malnutrition. India is often compared – and often compares itself – with China, but the fact is that as China became an economic powerhouse it greatly reduced malnutrition. In an all-fronts effort, China cut child malnutrition by two-thirds between 1990 and 2002. Today only 7 percent of Chinese children under age 5 are underweight, whereas the figure for India is 43 percent. Even in sub-Saharan Africa, which most people assume to have the direst poverty statistics, the average child-malnutrition rate is 28 percent.

The youthfulness that leaders like Ambani claim as the country's great competitive advantage could turn out to be the greatest stumbling block to Indian development and make it an also-ran to China. The science is disturbingly clear: if you are malnourished until age 3, your neural formation suffers, and most of that underdevelopment is fixed for life. […]

No one is quite sure why the nutrition situation in India is so dire. The lack of women's empowerment in both rural and urban areas is thought to play a major role. And so far, at least, the central government has been very slow to act. While India's per capita gross domestic product grew fourfold between 1992 and 2006 (the last period for which there are accurate statistics), the percentage of children age 3 and under who are underweight declined only to 46 percent from 52 nationally, and actually increased in some states.

It is not clear that those who live in this newly prosperous India even take in the depth of the nutrition crisis. The activist Harsh Mander told me it was possible for middle-class people to live in ignorance of the poor and to persuade themselves that poverty was not as bad as all that. There is a great deal of denial. Haddad said that when he asked Indian journalists what the malnutrition rate was, they consistently underestimated it by half and were often incredulous when told the actual figures. […]

[N.G.O.] activists are at least persuaded that the national government and many of the states are sincere in wanting to address malnutrition. In 2008, Prime Minister Singh declared under-nutrition "a curse we must remove," and he reaffirmed that commitment after his re-election. Moreover, it is almost certain that, after years of activist effort, a Right to Food Act will pass in Parliament. Most drafts call for a government-subsidized minimum of 25 kilograms (55 pounds) of food grain per family per month. There are enforcement provisions, the most important of which is that individual bureaucrats could be fined for failure. […]

Overcoming malnutrition requires not just an end to denial but also a decision that eradicating malnutrition is as much of a priority for India as its recent decision to build a hundred new ships for its navy over the next decade. Biraj Patnaik, a principal architect of the Right to Food campaign, is intransigent on the topic: "My question is if the government can spend 25 billion U.S. dollars on defense, why can't it spend an equivalent amount on ensuring the food security of the people of India?" Smiling, he added: "Of course it's a rhetorical question. I know perfectly well – we all know perfectly well – that neither the government this country now has or, for that matter, is ever likely to have, will ever lower the defense budget. But sometimes it's vital to ask rhetorical questions."
[…]

(870 words)

Abi Workshop Englisch
India Lehrerheft
ISBN 978-3-12-601016-0

Annotations

line 7: **Manmohan Singh** – the incumbent Prime Minister of India: he is the 14th Prime Minister of India, who returned to power in May 2009 after completing a full five-year term
line 24: **Goldman Sachs** – a global investment banking and securities firm
line 50: **also-ran** – a person who is not successful, especially in a competition or an election
line 55: **dire** – very serious, very bad
line 58/59: **gross domestic product (GDP)** – the total value of all the goods and services produced by a country in one year
line 74: **N.G.O. (non-governmental organisation)** – an organisation that is independent of government and business
line 91: **intransigent** – firm; not willing to change one's opinion or attitude

Tasks

1 Contents/Comprehension

a) Point out the change that India has undergone since the 1980s and find evidence in the text why the 21st century may indeed be India's.

b) Summarise the problem of malnutrition in India.

2 Form/Analysis

Explain the function of the last paragraph of this extract (ll. 86–100).

3 Comment/Text production

Child poverty is not only a problem of the developing countries but it is a serious issue in industrialised countries, too. Comment.

4 Translation

Read the article on page 98 and translate ll. 1–24 and ll. 42–46 into English.

Abi Workshop Englisch
India Lehrerheft
ISBN 978-3-12-601016-0

Dürre bremst Indiens Aufholjagd

Indiens schnelle Rückkehr zu hohen Wachstumsraten ist gefährdet. Grund dafür ist das Wetter. Asiens drittgrößter Wirtschaftsmacht droht die schlimmste Dürre seit zwei Jahrzehnten. Ökonomen senken bereits ihre Prognosen, die Börse nimmt das Unheil vorweg.

Neu Delhi. Während sich die Wirtschaft in vielen anderen Ländern langsam wieder erholt, droht Indien durch das Wetter weiter zurückzufallen. Bisher hat die Regenzeit, die lebenswichtig ist für die indische Landwirtschaft, ein Viertel weniger Niederschläge gebracht als im langjährigen Durchschnitt. [...]

Innerhalb weniger Wochen scheint der Optimismus der Ökonomen verflogen, wonach Indiens Wirtschaft nach zwei schwierigen Quartalen bald wieder bis zu sieben Prozent zulegen werde. Grund dafür ist die immense Bedeutung der Landwirtschaft für Indien. Obwohl sie nur knapp ein Fünftel zum Bruttoinlandsprodukt beiträgt, hängt an ihr das Wohlergehen von mehr als 500 Millionen Menschen. Der Agrarsektor war in den vergangenen Jahren eine maßgebliche Stütze des indischen Wirtschaftsbooms. Die Ernten waren gut, der Wohlstand auf dem Land stieg, plötzlich war Geld vorhanden für Konsumgüter wie Mobiltelefone, Motorräder und Fernseher.

Doch dieser Aufschwung steht und fällt mit den Launen des Monsuns, der den Großteil der jährlichen Regenfälle bringt und auch die Staudämme füllen muss, aus denen die Felder bewässert werden. Ist er schlecht, dann sind sofort Millionen Menschen vom Hunger bedroht. Verzweifelte Bauern erzielen keine Ernte mehr und müssen sich in die Fänge skrupelloser Geldverleiher begeben. Die Nahrungsmittelpreise steigen. Das dämpft auch die Konsumlust in den Städten, wo Lebensmittel ebenfalls den Großteil der meist kärglichen Einkommen aufzehren. Die Folgen der Dürre schlagen auf die gesamte Wirtschaft durch.

Die Börse in Bombay beginnt bereits, das drohende Unheil einzupreisen. Seit einigen Tagen fallen dort auf breiter Front die Kurse. " [...]

Lange hatte die Regierung in Neu-Delhi auf das Prinzip Hoffnung gesetzt, jetzt reagiert sie alarmiert.

Wenn nötig, werde es einschneidende Maßnahmen geben, um den Anstieg der Nahrungsmittelpreise abzufedern, sagte Premierminister Singh. Den Export von Reis und Weizen hat Indien bereits eingeschränkt, die Zölle für die Zuckereinfuhr ausgesetzt.

Weitere Eingriffe in den Handel zum Zweck der Preiskontrolle werden folgen. Sie haben in Indiens stark vom Staat gelenkten Wirtschaft Tradition.
[...]

(343 words)

Abi Workshop Englisch
India Lehrerheft
ISBN 978-3-12-601016-0

Klausurvorschlag Topic 4: Slumdog Millionaire (review)

by Sukhdev Sandhu

"Slumdog Millionaire" is an amazing film set in an equally amazing city, Mumbai.

Danny Boyle's "Slumdog Millionaire" is the film equivalent of Usain Bolt's performance at the Olympics: funny, shocking, spectacularly turbo-charged. It takes your breath away at the same time as it makes you want to holler with joy or to grab the person next to you: "Yes!"

Loosely adapted from Vikas Swarup's novel Q&A, the film is set in modern-day Mumbai. Like that city, it brims and overflows, chortles with multiplicity. It creates a scary and beguiling electricity by allowing opposites to collide – horror and joy, colourful fantasy and grimy reality, history and hyper-modernity. It is itself many different kinds of film: thriller, romance, picaresque, a Western stab at Bollywood.

It begins with Jamal Malik (Dev Patel […]) an 18-year-old call-centre chai-wallah, or tea-vendor, fluking his way onto the Indian version of "Who Wants To Be a Millionaire?" Here, though uneducated, and patronised by the show's host Prem Kumar (Anil Kapoor), he gets through round after round of questions to stand on the brink of winning the top prize.

No one can believe Jamal's success, though; he represents an India obscured by recent cheerleading about that country's growing affluence and middle-class swagger. He's seen as dirty, virtually untouchable.

Kumar, in a fit of pique, has local police officers headed by Irrfan Khan torture the young man. How, they want to know, pounding and electrocuting him as they interrogate him, can an upstart like him possibly know the answers to the TV show's questions?

And so, in a piece of plotting both nimble and schematic, one that involves lots of dramatic flashbacks, Malik reveals to the officers the train of events by which he amassed all sorts of facts.

He can answer a question about film actor Amitabh Bachchan because when he was younger he had dived into a public latrine in order to get the Bollywood legend's autograph. He can answer a question about a gun inventor because he'd heard the name "Colt" mentioned as he was helping his brother Salim to rescue fellow orphan Latika from the clutches of brutal pimps.

A fragmented biography emerges: he's a shanty-town urchin, born to a mother who's later slaughtered in an anti-Muslim pogrom, and forced to hustle a living that takes him on adventures both abysmal and exciting through a society that is becoming flashier and more urban as time goes by. […]

It's easy to sense the excitement that Boyle – and his cinematographer Anthony Dod Mantle – felt when shooting in Mumbai. They're alive to the jagged rhythms of the city, its palette of colours that are quite as rich and surreal as any in Trainspotting. […]

As such, "Slumdog Millionaire" strikes me as a hugely important film in contemporary cinema. It's an advertisement for the dramatic potential of the non-Western city. Mumbai, Chennai, Shanghai, Lagos: they, not New York or Los Angeles, over-familiar and culturally declining cities both, are where any writers and directors should be heading today. They offer more energy, extremity, humanity – fillips to the imagination.

Sure, there are risks involved for those who elect to make that kind of creative migration. These days any film set in a poor or developing nation will attract scrutiny.
What we now call the Third World was patronised or ignored by moviemakers for much of the 20th century; it's no bad thing if their successors are forced to think more deeply about what they're doing. […]

I've heard it said that "Slumdog Millionaire" itself is patronising, that it doesn't say enough about imperialism, that it prettifies suffering and poverty. To which I can only say: nonsense.

Boyle is not a political director, but his film is incalculably more radical than the glossy, blinged-out pictures that emerge every week from the studios of Mumbai. […]
"Slumdog Millionaire" is as acerbic as it is clear-eyed about the brutal power dynamics in modern-day Mumbai. But, at the same time, what makes it so warming and what has been inspiring audiences all across the world to cheer at its rousing ending, is its passion for a place that writer Suketu Mehta has described as a "maximum city".

Mumbai has been through hell recently. But "Slumdog Millionaire", whose everyman hero is a Muslim, is a wonderful tribute to it and to its people. It is, in fact, a maximum film.
Rating: *****

(712 words)

Abi Workshop Englisch
India Lehrerheft
ISBN 978-3-12-601016-0

Annotations

line 5: **Usain Bolt** – Usain "Lightning" Bolt, a 21-year-old Jamaican, took the 100 meter final in just 9.69 seconds in the 2008 Olympic Games in Beijing. Bolt crossed the line with his left shoelace coming loose.
line 13: **beguiling** – attractive and interesting but sometimes also mysterious
line 19: **chai** (IndE, infml) – tea
line 19: **wallah** (IndE, infml) – a person connected with a particular job
line 30: **pique** – annoyed or bitter feelings that you have, usually because your pride has been hurt
line 46: **pimp** – a man who controls prostitutes and lives on the money that they earn
line 47/48: **shanty town** – an area in or near a town where poor people live in small houses, built of pieces of wood, metal and cardboard
line 48: **urchin** – a young child who is poor and dirty, often one who has no home
line 50: **abysmal** – extremely bad or of a very low standard
line 70: **scrutiny** – careful and thorough examination
line 83: **acerbic** – critical in a direct and rather cruel way
line 90: **Mumbai has been through hell recently** – refers to the 2008 Mumbai attacks, more than ten coordinated shooting and bombing attacks across Mumbai carried out by a Pakistan-based terrorist organisation between November 26th and 29th, which left at least 173 people dead and more than 300 wounded

Tasks

1 Contents/Comprehension

a) Summarise the story line of Danny Boyle's film "Slumdog Millionaire".

b) According to the text, which role does Mumbai play in contemporary film making and in the making of "Slumdog Millionaire" in particular?

2 Form/Analysis

Analyse the author's opinion on the film and show how he uses language to illustrate his views.

3 Grammar

a) Rewrite the sentences without using a participle construction.

1. "Loosely adapted from Vikas Swarup's novel Q&A, the film is set in modern-day Mumbai." (ll. 10–11)
2. "It begins with Jamal Malik …, fluking his way onto the Indian version of 'Who Wants To Be a Millionaire?'" (ll. 18–21)

b) Put this statement of one of the actors in the film into reported speech. Use various introductory verbs in the simple past.
"Prior to the film I had never been to a slum before. Of course, before we started with the shooting, I went on location scouting to help me get into the character. I went to one slum called Tal Aviv, which has got a population of 2 million and still growing. Coming from London, I had this stupid preconceived notion, a stereotype of what a slum would be. When I went there, I was so happy to be proved wrong about what I had expected the slums to be. There was an overwhelming sense of community, everyone knows everyone and they're all working together in unison."

c) Change into the active voice.

1. "What we now call the Third World was patronised or ignored by moviemakers for much of the 20th century; …" (ll. 71–72)
2. "I've heard it said that 'Slumdog Millionaire' itself is patronising …" (ll. 75–76)

d) Complete these conditional sentences in accordance with the context.

1. If this film had been produced in Hollywood, …
2. If Jamal hadn't heard the name "Colt" when he was helping his brother Salim to rescue fellow orphan Latika from the clutches of brutal pimps, Jamal …

Abi Workshop Englisch
India Lehrerheft
ISBN 978-3-12-601016-0

e) Imagine you are working for a newspaper and your editor wants you to interview the director of "Slumdog Millionaire", Danny Boyle. Write down six interesting questions you would like to ask him in the interview.

4 Composition/Text production

"['Slumdog Millionaire'] is, in fact, a maximum film." (l. 93). Choose a book, film or play which you consider as "maximum" and write a review of it.

Abi Workshop Englisch
India Lehrerheft
ISBN 978-3-12-601016-0

Erwartungshorizont zu den Klausurvorschlägen

Topic 1: Textinformation (Text 1)

Autor:	Aravind Adiga
Titel:	The White Tiger
Quelle:	Free Press Subsidiary Rights Department, (A Division of Simon & Schuster, Inc.), 1230 Avenue of the Americas, New York, NY 10020, 2008, pp. 11–14.
Textformat/Textlänge:	Romanauszug, 1182 Wörter

Topic 1: Textinformation (Text 2)

Autor:	Charlotte Higgins
Titel:	Out of the Darkness: Adiga's White Tiger rides to Booker victory against the odds Published on Tuesday, 14 October 2008 by The Guardian online
Quelle:	http://www.guardian.co.uk/books/2008/oct/14/booker-prize-adiga-white-tiger/print (geprüft: 5.03.10)
Textformat/Textlänge:	Sachtext, 302 Wörter

Erwartungshorizont

1 Contents/Comprehension

a) India is "two countries in one"

- According to the narrator, there is an India of Light and an India of Darkness.
- All the places situated near the ocean are well off and thus lie in the light whereas those places near the Ganges, the black river, lie in darkness as the mud of the river "traps everything that is planted in it, suffocating and choking and stunting it" (ll. 13–14).

b) As a young child the narrator is attending his mother's funeral in the holy city of Benaras on the River Ganges. His grandmother Kusum, who the narrator characterises as sly and cunning (l. 55, l. 59), is leading the procession. His mother has been clad in expensive fine cloth which makes the narrator realise that "her death was so grand that I knew, all at once that her life must have been miserable" (ll. 69 ff). Down on the river bank, where the air was full of the smell of decaying flesh, pyres are being built and four bodies are already on fire. After logs of wood have been piled onto the corpse, the priest lights the body of the narrator's mother. However, when the flames reach the cloth, one of his mother's feet jerks out and although his grandmother shoves it back into the fire it will not burn, "like a living thing; the toes … offering resistance to what was being done to them" (ll. 103–106). For the narrator this sight is an indication of his mother's opposition to being and unwillingness to be destroyed (l. 108). He imagines that the thick black mud of the River Ganges makes her resist being swallowed by the river. The narrator at that moment realises that the river indeed is not "the breaker of the chain of birth and rebirth" (l. 33) and "the river of emancipation" (ll. 39 ff.), but the place "into which everything died, and decomposed, and was reborn from, and died into again … Nothing would get liberated here" (ll. 129–130). The narrator thus becomes disillusioned and loses his faith in the power of the River Ganges.

2 Form/Analysis

a) Explanation of phrases

- ponds … choked with lotuses and water lilies (ll. 19 ff.): small areas of still water which are blocked by and full of these tropical plants
- … and urge you to take a dip in it (l. 43): … and try hard to persuade you to immerse yourself in it
- a giant oozing mound of black mud (ll. 110 ff.): a huge pile of dark, wet, soft and sticky earth flowing slowly from one place to another

b) Analysis of narrative perspective and its effect

- The story is presented in letter form from a first-person limited point of view.

Abi Workshop Englisch
India Lehrerheft
ISBN 978-3-12-601016-0

- The narrator addresses the recipient of his letters directly ("Mr. Premier", l. 15; "Please understand, Your Excellency", that India is two countries in one", l. 22–23; "No! – Mr. Jiabao, I urge you not to dip in the Ganga", l. 44) which makes the passages vivid and immediate.
- The narrator relates personal experiences (here the funeral procession) but also provides background information (e.g. here the importance of the River Ganges in the Hindu religion) and includes asides criticising India's politics (here his criticism of the false statements of the Indian prime minister).
- The narrator provides a very graphic and detailed and yet at the same time rather detached description of the events at the river Ganges as if he was merely an observer and not really a close relative partaking in the funeral procession, thus leaving the evaluation of the scene to the reader.

Analysis of style and its effect

- simple sentence structure
  mostly short main clauses; coordinated clauses linked with "and" or "but" or without connective devices; only few relative clauses or participle constructions; effect: like written speech; vivid and immediate
- imagery and figures of speech
  light and darkness (l. 13–14; ll. 21 ff.): illustrates the "two Indias";
  personification: "Mother Ganga, daughter of the Vedas, river of illumination, protector of us all, breaker of the chain of birth and rebirth" (ll. 31 ff.): shows the importance of the river Ganges in the Hindu religion;
  climax: "whose grip traps everything that is planted in it, suffocating and choking and stunting it" (ll. 29–30): emphasises the destructive effect of the mud of the river, an image that is taken up by a repetition at the end of the extract: "She was trying to fight the black mud; … but the mud was sucking her in, sucking her in" (ll. 118 ff.)

3 Comment/Text production

a) How foreign tourists should behave in order not to violate the feelings of the local population – possible aspects

- When Western tourists visit remote villages in less developed countries, people with very different cultural values are brought into contact with each other. This frequently leads to culture shock, friction and misunderstandings.
  Tourists often commit social faux pas out of ignorance of how to behave appropriately.
- Thus before they start their journey, tourists should inform themselves on the dos and don'ts relevant in the country/countries they are going to visit in order to behave appropriately.
- In some countries, for example, hugging or kissing in public is considered offensive.
- Smoking or consuming alcohol publicly might also cause offense.
- In some cultures men only socialise with men, and women only with women; thus casual conversations with a member of the opposite sex might be considered as inappropriate.
- Tourists should avoid taking too intrusive photographs in order not to violate the locals' feelings.
- It is vital to wear appropriate clothes, particularly at religious places.

b) Could you personally imagine spending your holidays in India? *Individuelle S-Antworten.*

4 Mediation

Nach einem hart umkämpften Jury-Durchgang gewann Aravind Adiga den Man Booker Preis für seinen Debüt-Roman „The White Tiger" – einem Roman über die Schattenseiten des modernen Indien. „The White Tiger" analysiert die Realität hinter Indiens Wirtschaftswunder. Durch Lügen und Betrug schafft der Erzähler Balram Hjalwai den Aufstieg in Bangalores Geschäftswelt. Der Roman hat seinen Ursprung in der Tätigkeit des Autors als Journalist und dessen Begegnungen mit Mitgliedern der indischen Unterschicht. Auch wenn die Leute sich nicht für die sozialen Unterschiede interessieren, sind diese nach Ansicht des Autors ein enormes Problem, weil z.B. Terrorismus und Instabilität daraus hervorgehen. Das Buch war in Indien außerordentlich erfolgreich. Nach Einschätzung des Autors verschwindet die früher existierende gemeinsame Kultur zwischen den Armen und den Reichen immer mehr.
Der Vorsitzende der Preisrichter hebt hervor, dass es Adiga gelingt, die Aufmerksamkeit für einen Helden zu gewinnen, der ein kompromissloser Bösewicht ist. Die sozialen Themen, die in diesem Buch im Mittelpunkt stehen, machen es sehr lesenswert.

Abi Workshop Englisch
India Lehrerheft
ISBN 978-3-12-601016-0

Topic 2: Textinformation

Autor: Amelia Gentleman
Titel: 'The Queen's Hinglish' gains in India
Published on Wednesday, November 21, 2007 by The New York Times online
Quelle: http://www.nytimes.com/2007/11/21/world/asia/21iht-letter.1.8417733.html?scp=1&sq=The%20Queen's%20Hinglish%20gains%20in%20India&st=cse
(geprüft: 5.03.2010)
Textformat/Textlänge: Sachtext, 726 Wörter

Erwartungshorizont

1 Contents/Comprehension

a) The role of English in today's India in contrast to the past

- In the past the characteristics of the Indian variety of English were ridiculed and sneered at.
- However, the authors of the three recently published books point out how important the blend of English and Hindi has become in modern India, with more people speaking English "in South Asia than in Britain and North America combined, with India alone accounting for more than 350 million English speakers" (ll. 40–42).
- Instead of feeling ashamed or even inferior to people speaking Received Pronunciation, speakers of Hinglish use their language freely and are "becoming more and more comfortable with mixing words from languages such as Hindi, Urdu, Punjabi with English" (ll. 43–45) whereas in the past this blending of different languages was criticised by linguistic purists.
- Rather than being considered as a means of communication of the uneducated masses as it was in the past, Hinglish has become fashionable and is now considered "the language of the movers and shakers" (ll. 58 ff).

b) Why the role of Indian English has changed and how it will develop in the future

- Because of India's economic success as well as rising national self esteem Indians have become proud of Indian English (ll. 10–11); according to V. Narang, a linguistics professor at Delhi's JNU University, increasing wealth has led to more self-confidence "in ourselves and our language" (l. 67).
- The media, i.e. newspapers and television, make use of Hinglish and thus spread Indian English.
- In the future Indian English could become a variety of English which is accepted worldwide (ll. 31–33) and "the most widely spoken form of English on earth" (ll. 49–50); it is predicted that "Indian English is certainly likely to become more and more powerful" (ll. 88–89).

2 Form/Analysis

a) Explain these phrases as they are used in the text

- Ill-concealed smirking at the peculiarities of Indian English has long been a handy fallback … (ll. 1–2): quite openly ridiculing the oddities of Indian English has long been a comfortable course of action.
- Hinglish, once seen as the lingo of the uneducated masses, is now trendy – the language of the movers and shakers (ll. 57–58): Hinglish, which used to be considered the language of the great number of people with little or no formal school education, has now become fashionable among people with power and influence.

b) Explain the function of the headline 'The Queen's Hinglish' gains in India

- First of all the word "Hinglish", a blending of the words "Hindi" and "English", points to the content of the article – the reader at once becomes aware that the article must be about the interrelationship between the two languages in India; the verb "gains" refers to the fact that Indian English is becoming more and more important in India.
- The headline thus sums up the main focus of the article.
- At the same time the headline arouses the reader's interest by juxtaposing the noun Queen with Hinglish, thus leaving the reader to wonder about the connection between these words.

Abi Workshop Englisch
India Lehrerheft
ISBN 978-3-12-601016-0

3 Composition/Text production

Point out the role of the English language in our globalised world – possible aspects

- English is the most widely spoken language by non-natives in the world
- English has become a global lingua franca; it is relevant and sometimes even obligatory in various fields, for example in science and technology, international business, international politics (English is one of the official languages of the United Nations) and diplomacy, aviation or entertainment.
- English is a vital means of communication via the Internet.
- Being proficient in the English language has now become a necessary prerequisite for job applicants in the whole world; lack of English language skills will put people at a considerable disadvantage in education, at work and particularly in the field of technological advances.
- English has had and still has a huge impact on the development of other languages as speakers often take over English expressions which eventually become part of the national vocabulary.
- Wherever one may travel today one is very likely to meet someone who can converse in English.

Topic 3: Textinformation (Text 1)

Autor:	David Rieff
Titel:	India's malnutrition dilemma
	Published on Thursday, October 8, 2009 by The New York Times online
Quelle:	http://www.nytimes.com/2009/10/11/magazine/11FOB-Rieff-t.html?sq=women%20in%20india&st=cse&scp=12&pagewanted=print October 11, 2009 (geprüft: 5.03.2010)
Textformat/Textlänge:	Sachtext, 870 Wörter

Topic 3: Textinformation (Text 2)

Autor:	Helmut Hauschild
Titel:	Dürre bremst Indiens Aufholjagd
Quelle:	Published on Tuesday, August 11, 2009 by Handelsblatt online http://www.handelsblatt.com/politik/konjunktur-nachrichten/duerre-bremst-indiens-aufholjagd;2443595 (geprüft: 5.03.2010)
Textformat/Textlänge:	Sachtext, 343 Wörter

Erwartungshorizont

1 Contents/Comprehension

a) Point out the change that India has undergone since the 1980s and find evidence in the text

- India's economy is booming: between 1992 and 2006 the GDP grew fourfold (l. 58–59), thus fundamentally changing the face of India, which only in the late 1980s had an economy "in which it was said you needed the intercession of a member of Parliament just to get a telephone line." (ll. 16–17)
- This economic success enables the Indian middle-class, which seems to be confident about its country's prospects (ll. 22–23), to lead a life as comparably comfortable as their counterparts in Shanghai or Berlin (ll. 18–19).
- Economy experts and industrialists believe that the 21st century will be India's, particularly because of its favourable age structure: India's young population is in contrast to "the ageing populations of the United States, Western Europe, Japan and China." (ll. 33 ff.)

b) Summarise the problem of malnutrition in India

- In India the child-malnutrition rate is 43 %, surpassing even sub-Saharan Africa (28 %).
- Being underweight in early childhood has fundamental consequences for the child and its development: "If you are malnourished until age 3, your neural formation suffers, and most of that underdevelopment is fixed for life." (ll. 51–53)
- Obviously members of the economically blossoming middle-class often deny the seriousness of the child-malnutrition problem or are totally ignorant of the facts; Indian journalists, for instance, "consistently

Abi Workshop Englisch
India Lehrerheft
ISBN 978-3-12-601016-0

underestimated [the malnutrition rate] by half and were often incredulous when told the actual figures." (ll. 71–73)
- So far the state government has done little to address the problem (l. 57–58); there are, however, serious promises by the government and many of the Indian states to tackle the issue (ll. 86 ff.).

2 Form/Analysis

- In this paragraph the author of the article points out that the problem of malnutrition can only be solved if overcoming the problem is equally important to the government as "its recent decision to build a hundred new ships for its navy over the next decade" (ll. 88 ff).
- The author quotes one of the founders of the Right to Food campaign, Biraj Patnaik, to support his view. Patnaik in a rhetorical question asks why the government cannot spend an equally high sum on providing enough food for the Indian population as it does on defense. He then goes to explain that neither the present nor any prospective future Indian government will decrease the budget on defense. He insists, however, that "sometimes it is vital to ask rhetorical questions" (ll. 99–100).
- Thus this paragraph makes the reader wonder why indeed it is not possible for the Indian government to reduce spending on defense and instead spend more money on tackling the problem of malnutrition. So these lines are aimed at convincing the reader of the author's opinion pointed out in ll. 86–90.

3 Comment/Text production

Possible aspects
- Despite persistent economic growth and remarkable improvements in the standard of living in industrialised nations throughout the twentieth century, a significant percentage of children are still living below the poverty line, which threatens their physical and psychological development and well-being as well as their future.
- E.g. in the United States almost one in five children lives in poverty; the rate for Canada is one in 7 and 9.1 percent of all children in Germany are considered poor (2007).
- Child poverty is not only a matter of a low living standard; these children are often deprived of preschool education, necessary medical check-ups and cannot enjoy ordinary free-time activities like going to the cinema, having an ice-cream with their friends or visiting the zoo.
- Thus these children often face health, behavioral as well as emotional problems.
- Children who live below the poverty-line often attain lower levels of education which puts them at a disadvantage when they start their career, thus they are more likely to live in poverty as adults in comparison to those children who have enjoyed a decent living standard.
- Thus child poverty is a serious social problem, not only in developing but also in industrialised countries and governments must make a serious effort to reduce child poverty and alleviate its consequences.

4 Translation

Drought slows down India's race to catch up
India's quick return to high growth rates is at risk. The reason for this is the weather. Asia's third largest economic power is threatened by the most serious drought in two decades. Economists are already lowering their prognoses, the stock exchange is anticipating the disaster.
New Delhi. While the economy in many countries is slowly recovering, India is at risk of falling further behind. Until now the rainy season, which is vital for India's agriculture, has brought less than a quarter of the average amount of rainfall. […]
Within a few weeks, the optimism of the economists seems to have vanished, according to which India's economy was going to grow up to seven percent after two difficult quarters. The reason for this is the great importance of agriculture for India's economy. Although it only accounts for one fifth of the gross domestic product, the well-being of more than 500 million people depends on it. The agricultural sector has been a significant pillar of India's economic boom. Harvests were good, wealth in the countryside grew, suddenly there was money available for consumer goods like cellular phones, motorcycles and television sets. […]
If necessary, drastic measures will be taken in order to mitigate the rise in food prices, said Prime Minister Singh. India has already curtailed the export of rice and wheat and suspended customs duty on the import of sugar.

Abi Workshop Englisch
India Lehrerheft
ISBN 978-3-12-601016-0

Topic 4: Textinformation

Autor: Sukhdev Sandhu
Titel: Slumdog Millionaire, review
Published on Thursday, January 8, 2009 by The Telegraph
Quelle: http://www.telegraph.co.uk/culture/film/filmreviews/4176184/Slumdog-Millionaire-review.html (geprüft: 5.03.2010)
Textformat/Textlänge: Rezension, 712 Wörter

Erwartungshorizont

1 Contents/Comprehension

a) Story line of Danny Boyle's film

- 18-year-old Jamal Malik, who earns his living in a call-centre selling tea, is very close to winning the top prize in the Indian version of "Who Wants To Be a Millionaire?".
- Despite the fact that Jamal is uneducated and grew up as a poor child in a shanty town, he is able to answer all the host's questions although he treats him rather condescendingly.
- Jamal, who is considered "as dirty, virtually untouchable" (l. 29) arouses suspicion as "no one can believe Jamal's success" (l. 26).
- The show's host, who is obviously annoyed and embittered about Jamal's success, has local police officers interrogate him; these officers torture Jamal in their attempt to find out how Jamal could possibly know the answer to all the questions in the TV show.
- Jamal relates all the adventures and experiences he has had which have eventually resulted in this knowledge.

b) Role of Mumbai

- **In contemporary film making**
  According to the text, Mumbai and other non-Western cities like Chennai, Shanghai or Lagos are the places contemporary film-makers should be going today, as they "offer more energy, extremity, humanity – fillips to the imagination" (ll. 65–66) in comparison to western cities like New York or Los Angeles, which are too familiar and culturally going downhill (ll. 62–63).

- **In the making of "Slumdog Millionaire"**
  - "Slumdog Millionaire" resembles its setting as the film, similar to Mumbai, "brims and overflows, chortles with multiplicity" (l. 12), i.e. it is full of and joyfully spills over with a great variety.
  - The film relentlessly shows the grim reality of Mumbai: it is "as acerbic as it is clear-eyed about the brutal power dynamics of modern-day Mumbai" (ll. 84–85), but at the same time praises its setting and in fact shows its respect for the city which had to face disastrous terrorist attacks only recently (l. 90).
  - Just as Mumbai is a "maximum city" (l. 89), "Slumdog Millionaire" is a "maximum film" (l. 93), thus resembling once again the city itself.

2 Form/Analysis

- The author is thrilled by "Slumdog Millionaire" and considers it "a hugely important film in contemporary cinema" (l. 59).
- The author reveals his attitude toward the film by the very strong adjectives he uses to describe "Slumdog Millionaire", e.g. "funny, shocking, spectacularly turbo-charged" (l. 6).
- The author often compares the film to the city of Mumbai and points out that "like that city, it brims and overflows, chortles with multiplicity" (l. 12).
- He also employs contrast in order to illustrate the contrasts inherent in the film (ll. 14 ff.).
- The author dismisses critics of the film in a rather straightforward way: he simply writes: "To which I can only say: nonsense" (l. 78).
- The author is very outspoken and frank in his view on the film, which also becomes obvious in the last paragraphs, in which he emphasises his appraisal of the movie by again using strong attributes (acerbic, clear-eyed, a wonderful tribute, a maximum film, ll. 83 ff.).

ISBN 978-3-12-601016-0

3 Grammar

a) 1. The film, which is loosely adapted from Vikas Swarup's novel Q&A, is set in modern-day Mumbai.
2. It begins with Jamal Malik …, who flukes his way onto the Indian version of "Who Wants To Be a Millionaire"?

b) The actor pointed out that prior to the film he had never been to a slum before. Of course, before they had stated with the shooting, he had gone on location scouting to help him get into the character. He mentioned that he had gone to one slum called Tal Aviv, which had got a population of 2 million and was still growing. Coming from London, he had had this stupid preconceived notion, a stereotype of what a slum would be. But he explained that when he had gone there, he had been so happy to be proved wrong about what he had expected the slums to be. Obviously there had been an overwhelming sense of community, everyone knew everyone and they were all working together in unison.

c) 1. Moviemakers patronised and ignored what we now call the Third World for much of the 20th century …
2. I've heard people say that Slumdog Millionaire itself is patronising …

d) 1. If this film had been produced in Hollywood, it might not have been as authentic as it actually turned out to be.
2. If Jamal hadn't heard the name "Colt" when he was helping his brother Salim to rescue fellow orphan Latika from the clutches of brutal pimps, Jamal might not have been able to answer the question about a gun inventor.

e) 1. Why did you decide to produce the film in Mumbai rather than in Hollywood?
2. Do you think that the film will be more successful in India than in Europe or America?
3. Did you find it difficult to get adequate actors for the different roles in the film?
4. Critics have argued that the film prettified suffering and poverty – what's your attitude towards this reproach?
5. Which similarities and which differences do you see if you compare "Slumdog Millionaire" to the typical Bollywood films?
6. What kind of film are you planning to produce next?

4 Composition/Text production

In general

- In a review a text, an event, an object, or a phenomenon is critically analysed. It is vital that the author of a review presents an argument. Thus students must make sure that their review is not merely a summary but is a commentary on the book, film or play that they have chosen to write about.

In general, reviews contain three different parts

- First, a review gives the reader a concise summary of the content.
- Second, and more importantly, a review offers a critical assessment of the content. This involves the author's reactions to the work under review: what strikes him/her as noteworthy, whether or not it was effective or persuasive, and how it enhanced one's understanding of the issues at hand.
- Finally, a review often offers a recommendation and suggests whether or not the audience would appreciate it.

Points to be considered when evaluating the students' reviews

- Does the review have a clear structure, e.g. a thesis statement, supporting body paragraphs, and a conclusion?
- As the topic asks students to focus on a "maximum" book, film or play, does the text contain convincing arguments to support the author's opinion that the piece is indeed exceptional and extraordinary? Is the author's opinion delivered in a clear, concise manner?
- Does the text combine balanced opinion and concrete examples? Do the specific examples back up the author's assertions in a convincing way?
- Does the text offer a recommendation to a potential audience?
- Does the author present a balanced and fair argument about the value of the book, play or film.

Abi Workshop Englisch
India Lehrerheft
ISBN 978-3-12-601016-0

Erwartungshorizont zu den *Revision files*

Revision file 1: A plural country

geographical

- huge cities with approximately 5–12 million inhabitants
- rural areas
- three major geographical regions

ethnic

- differences in descent

diversity

social

- vast number of different languages and dialects and English as a lingua franca
- differences in customs, taste, cuisine
- differences in dress, colour, costume
- caste system

religious

- Hindu faith adhered to by 4/5th of population
- India is home to every religion known to mankind
- ever-present spirituality

Unity

- shared history: India has emerged from an ancient civilisation
- India as a secular pluralistic state
- one land embracing many
- strong belief in the principles of democracy

– unity in diversity –

Abi Workshop Englisch
India Lehrerheft
ISBN 978-3-12-601016-0

Revision file 2: The wounds of history

Describe the social and political problems India faces today.

Muslims in India	Pakistan	International relations
– Muslims face bad socio-economic conditions: problems of disenfranchisement, poverty, unemployment and systemic discrimination, poor housing and poor education as well as illiteracy and high crime rates. – The series of terrorist attacks in Mumbai in November 2008 has been attributed to Muslims in Pakistan but has led to suspicion towards Muslims in India who are branded as anti-national, terrorists and agents of Pakistan. – Thus Muslims live in a sense of despair and suspicion. – Economic, social and political discontent are catalysts for radicalism and thus there is a potential threat to the national security of India.	– Pakistan is accused by India of having supported the 2008 Mumbai terrorist attacks. – Since 1947, when the two new states India and Pakistan were founded, Kashmir has been a constant source of tension between the two countries. – The partition of India and the creation of two states, India and Pakistan, was and is still considered an unnecessary tragedy by many Indians who think that partition neglected India's natural geographical and cultural boundaries and thus should be rectified eventually. – Pakistan is considered an existential threat to India's secular identity with the potential of averting the loyalty of India's Muslim minority. – The extreme fear of their Indian neighbours seems to emanate predominantly from the Pakistani government and military; direct interaction between ordinary Indians and Pakistanis is usually characterised by mutually friendly feelings towards each other.	– The world has glossed over India's problems (cf. quote by former US Defense Secretary Cohen: US and India as "perfect partners" because of their "multiethnic and secular democracies"). – People like Pankaj Mishra believe that Churchill's support of the Muslims in India was one of the factors contributing to the growth of international Muslim terrorism, a "global jihad" involving attacks like 09/11.

Now try to link the present situaion with historical events / developments. The following keywords might help you: partition • Jinnah • Gandhi • viceroy • World War II • …

British Raj (1858–1947) = British rule in India (viceroy): World War II fundamentally weakened GB which had gradually lost control over the subcontinent in the 1940s.

Jinnah; founder of "The Muslim League" and the driving force behind the creation of Pakistan as a Muslim state.

Strong rejection of the idea of a separate Muslim territory by the Congress
→ Violence between Muslims and Hindus ensued

Mahatma Gandhi: philosophy of civil disobedience against British authority; founder of the "Quit India" movement aimed at the withdrawal of British troops from India

Independence and partition of predominantly Muslim regions of north into separate nation of Pakistan by Lord Mountbatten, the last viceroy
→ India was partitioned along religious lines
→ Armed conflict over rival claims to Bengal, Punjab, Jammu and Kashmir
→ Three wars between India and Pakistan; third one (1971) resulted in creation of Bangladesh

Show/Visualise the relations between the different events by drawing arrows.

Abi Workshop Englisch
India Lehrerheft
ISBN 978-3-12-601016-0

Revision file 3: Different worlds

Collect key information about different groups in India and fill the appropriate boxes.
Then think about the implications for the future.

Rural population

- simple housing
- physically strenuous work (simple means, manual labour)
- child labour
- no or difficult access to public amenities and services
- mass migration to the cities
- worsening living standard due to the rising demand for water by the urban population

Urban population

- bustling city life
- crowded and densely-populated mega-cities
- modern housing and offices (high-rise buildings)
- western-style malls and huge industrial parks
- huge gap between the wealthy and the middle-class and the poor
- huge number of people living below the poverty-level (shanty towns, bad sanitation, street children)
- not enough affordable housing and regular jobs for rural migrants → animosities, fierce competition

Hopes and challenges for the future:

- establishing and maintaining social equality
- solving problems of energy and water supply, education, health care, sanitation and environmental pollution both in rural and urban areas
- economic success must improve lives of both rural and urban population alike, must not deepen gap between rich and poor in India

Abi Workshop Englisch
India Lehrerheft
ISBN 978-3-12-601016-0

Revision file 4: East meets West

In (the texts of) this chapter you have learnt that East and West interact in different ways. Name facts from the texts that show Eastern influence on the West and the other way round.

East goes West

- men and women of Indian origin reaching top positions in the West in education, business, research, fashion and arts
- Indian film industry (Bollywood), Indian literature, food, fashion, lifestyle and art have huge impact on the West
- Indian culture, spiritualism, exoticism and sensuality are successful exports from India

West goes East

- westerners go East in search for "software" like knowledge, services, ideas and concepts
- English spreads in the East as a unifying language of a permanently diverse Indian people
- outsourcing: Western firms rely on Indian call centres employing Indians trained to speak with an authentic American accent

What role does Eastern influence play in your life?

Eastern influence in my life

Individuelle S-Beiträge.

Abi Workshop Englisch
India Lehrerheft
ISBN 978-3-12-601016-0